Weapons for Spiritual Warfare

Applying spiritual weapons that will cause massive destruction to the kingdom of darkness

Revised and Expanded Version
(Large Print)

Angela Holloway

Weapons for Spiritual Warfare Revised and Expanded Version: Applying Spiritual Weapons That Will Cause Massive Destruction to the Kingdom of Darkness by Angela Holloway

Copyright © 2013, 2018 by Angela Holloway
All rights reserved

This book or parts thereof may not be reproduced in any form, stored in a retrieval system, or transmitted in any form by any means–electronic, mechanical, photocopy, recording, or otherwise –without prior written permission of the author and publisher, except as provided by United States of America copyright law.

Published by Angela Holloway

Cover Design by Angela Holloway
Cover image provided by Joseph Massey –www.joefloridaledlights.com

Except otherwise noted, Scripture references are taken from the *King James Version* of the Bible.

Scripture quotations marked (AMP) are taken from the *Amplified Bible*, Copyright © 1954, 1958, 1962, 1964, 1965, 1987 by The Lockman Foundation. Used by permission.

Scripture quotations marked Message are taken from *The Message: The Bible in Contemporary Language*, Large Print Numbered Edition, Eugene H. Peterson, Copyright © 2002, 2005 Used by Permission of NavPress Publishing Group, Colorado Springs, Colorado, All Rights Reserved. www.navpress.com.

Previous ISBN: 978-0-615-80039-4   (2013) *Weapons for Spiritual Warfare: Applying Spiritual Weapons That Will Cause Massive Destruction to the Kingdom of Darkness* published by Angela Holloway:

ISBN (2018) Revised and Expanded Version: 978-0-692-09214-9

Printed in the United States of America

 Contents

Acknowledgements 6

My Prayer 7

INTRODUCTION: Warfare 8

    1. Review Questions 21

CHAPTER ONE: The Weapon of Prayer 23

    1. Prayer is the Weapon that Called the Elements
       to Attention 26

    2. Prayer is the Weapon that caused Hezekiah to Cancel
       the Assignment of the enemy 35

    3. Intercessory prayer gave Peter a get out of jail free
       card and Daniel spiritual revelation and
       understanding 44

    4. Review Questions 51

CHAPTER TWO: The Weapon of the Word 56

    1. Why describe the Word of God as Indispensable
       and a Sword 57

    2. The Word Weapon Indentified as the
       Sword of the Spirit 64

    3. The Spoken Word in Spiritual Warfare 66

    4. The Spoken Word against the Spirit of Infirmity 68

    5. The Spoken Word against the Spirits of
       Lack and Bondage 74

    6. Jesus and the Weapon of the Word of God 81

    7. Review Questions 88

 Contents

CHAPTER THREE: The Weapon of the Name of Jesus 93
   1. There is life in Jesus' Name for Those who Believe 94
   2. There is Faith and Salvation in the Name of Jesus 96
   3. The Name of Jesus is the Way to Salvation 97
   4. Power in the name of Jesus 101
   5. Power at the Mention of the Name of Jesus 107
   6. No Greater name than the Name of Jesus 111
   7. Review Questions 113

CHAPTER FOUR: The Weapon of the Blood 118
   1. Remission, Cleansing, and Redemption of sins 124
   2. Reconciliation and Peace 128
   3. The Blood of Jesus Covers 130
   4. Review Questions 138

CHAPTER FIVE: The Weapon of Praise 143
   1. Send Judah First: the meaning and characteristics of Praise 146
   2. The Ram's horn trumpet and a Shout 149
   3. Send anointed Praisers and God will fight the battle 152
   4. Praise Destroys the Spirit of Heaviness 155
   5. Praise Opens Prison Doors 156
   6. Review Questions 161

Contents

CHAPTER SIX: The Weapon of Fasting 166

    1. The Improper Way to Fast 168

    2. The Proper Way to Fast 170

    3. Fasting as a weapon in Spiritual Warfare 174

    4. Fasting against Personal and National Annihilation 178

    5. Review Questions 187

CHAPTER SEVEN: The Weapon of Love 193

    1. The Mature Love of Jesus 194

    2. Flowing in Mature Love 195

    3. What Mature Love Does 196

    4. Love repels Hatred 198

    5. Love repels Jealousy 202

    6. Review Questions 208

CHAPTER EIGHT: The Weapon of Forgiveness 214

    1. Jesus Operates in the Weapon of Forgiveness 216

    2. Joseph Operated in the Weapon of Forgiveness 222

    3. Review Questions 235

CONCLUSION: We Win! 242

    1. Review Questions 246

Notes 248

Book Purchase Contact Information 250

Book Purchase Order Form 251

Acknowledgements

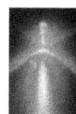

I give all the glory and honor to my Heavenly Father, my Savior, Lord, King, Best friend, Big Brother Jesus, and my Best friend the Holy Spirit for using me as the Vessel to write this book.

To my husband, David, thank you for your support and being a great reader. I love and appreciate you so much.

To my children, Simone and Sierra, I love you. Thank you both for your support and reading for me.

To Elder Aletra Parsons and Teacher Michelle Coe, thank you both for being readers for me. I truly appreciate you taking the time out of your busy schedules to assist me.

To Open Door Ministries, thank you all for your support and encouragement regarding this book. You are some of the best people in the kingdom of God and I will not take it back! I love you all very much and consider it an honor to serve as one of your Senior Pastors.

To the body of Christ and the kingdom of God as a whole, this book is for you.

My Prayer

Father, in the name of Jesus, I pray that every word in this book will be anointed and relevant penetrating the hearts and minds of everyone who reads it. I pray the Word of God will quicken the person(s) spirit and the pages will come alive giving every person reading a clear understanding and revelation knowledge of spiritual warfare with simplicity. I pray that every believer will embrace that through Jesus we have already received the victory. I pray that the Holy Spirit will revive and renew a fire in every believer to become a kingdom warrior. Holy Spirit, I also ask that you overflow supernatural power in the believers' inner beings to boldly apply every spiritual weapon mentioned in this book effectively against the kingdom of Satan and the power and influences of darkness producing manifested results in their lives and for the kingdom of God. Father, I ask that you do this for your glory in Jesus' name. Thank you and Amen.

Introduction

Warfare

For though we walk (live) in the flesh, we are not carrying on our warfare according to the flesh and using mere human weapons. For the weapons of our warfare are not physical weapons of flesh and blood, but they are mighty before God for the overthrow and destruction of strongholds (2 Corinthians 10:3-4, AMP Version).

In the body of Christ, spiritual warfare is an absolute whether we preach about it or not; therefore, believers should be equipped for the warfare. Warfare is war which is armed conflict or aggression. It entails action or an aggressive military deed; battle or military fight; campaign or an attack to win; carnage or massacre/annihilation; combat or battle; contest or fight and struggle; and defense or armament to protect.[1] In the United States government, the natural military is an organized system of branches strategically designed to equip soldiers for war. The soldiers are taught how to attack enemies by air (Air Force), land (Army and Marines), and sea (Navy and Coast Guard). Each branch is organized with a chain of command from the lowest ranking soldier to General with the President

---

[1.] *Roger's 21st Century Thesaurus*, 3rd ed. Philip Lief Group, s.v. "warfare," accessed December 20, 2010, http://thesaurus.com/browse/warfare?

as Commander in Chief. If an enemy of the nation is antagonistic or hostile opposing our country,[2] the Generals begin to immediately devise a plan of defense with the Commander in Chief. Upon approval, the Generals relay the information down the chain of command and put it into combat action. In turn, there is a campaign defense where the soldiers use military weapons and armor to carnage the enemy in the natural warfare.

In spiritual warfare, believers have an antagonistic enemy like the the natural military has an antagonistic enemy. However, the major difference is "we are not carrying our warfare in the flesh" because our fight is against spiritual beings (Satan and his cohorts) in the spirit realm. In addition, like the natural military has a chain of command, believers have one as well with God the Father, God the Son, and God the Holy Spirit as our Commander in Chief.

God the Father has given all power and authority to God the Son. God the Son defeated Satan and his cohorts triumphing openly over them and gave authority and power to the believers through God the Holy Spirit. Therefore, believers have the approval of our Commander in Chief

---

[2.] *Dictionary.com Unabridged*, Random House Inc, s.v. "antagonism," accessed December 20, 2010, http://dictionary.reference.com/browse/antagonism.

to be equipped and engaged in combat action to carnage Satan and his cohort's activities. This is important because the activities of the battle performed in the spirit realm affects the natural realm of the believer's life.

The Bible speaks about believers engaging in warfare as soldiers. In the natural military soldiers are required to separate themselves from civilian life in order to be focused, trained, and equipped to become soldiers with the ability to serve our country. This type of dedication requires discipline. Like the natural military, Paul encourages the servants of the Gospel to endure hardness as a good soldier of Jesus and be disciplined separating ourselves from the affairs of the world or "this life." This type of discipline is essential for a believer chosen by God in our warfare to please God (2 Timothy 2: 3-4). Additionally, Paul encourages spiritual soldiers to stand alert, in truth, faith, deliverance, living right before God, operating through/in the Spirit, and fortified in the Word of God as part of the uniform armor for battle against Satan and his organized chain of cohorts (Ephesians 6:11-17, AMP Version).

Put on God's whole armor (the armor of a heavy-armed soldier which God supplies), that you may be able to successfully to stand up against all the strategies and the deceits of the devil (11).

For we are not wrestling with flesh and blood (contending only with physical opponents), but against the despotisms, against the powers, against the master spirits who are the world rulers of this present darkness, against the spirit forces of wickedness in the heavenly (supernatural) sphere (12).

Therefore, put on God's complete armor, that you may be able to resist and stand your ground on the evil day of danger, and having done all the crisis demands, to stand firmly in your place (13).

Stand therefore (hold your ground), having tightened the belt of truth around your loins and having put on the breastplate of integrity and of moral rectitude and right standing with God (14).

And having shod your feet in preparation to face the enemy with the firm-footed stability, the promptness, and the readiness produced by the good news of the Gospel of peace (15).

Lift up over all the covering shield of saving faith, upon which you can quench all the flaming missiles of the wicked one (16).

And take the helmet of salvation and the sword that the Spirit wields, which is the Word of God (17).

Based on the text, it is evident that believers must have the proper armor in order to be armed and ready to stand in the operation of spiritual warfare. It also reveals that believers are required to function in God's supernatural abilities, weapons, and strength to hold our ground in spiritual warfare.

In this hour, believers must be taught the importance of spiritual warfare. The subject has either been presented too difficult for believers to apprehend or Satan is presented as a non-threat to believers. Some preachers are teaching that we should not speak about Satan because we are giving him praise to talk about his agenda. That type of teaching is deceptive. Peter cautions us to be sober of mind and vigilant at all times for our enemy the devil (Satan) roams around like a lion seeking someone to seize upon and devour (1 Peter 5:8, AMP Version). In the text, the words sober and vigilant challenge believers to be alert and watching out for Satan's agenda against our lives, families, ministries, and destinies because his desire is to destroy and devour any accessible person.

Therefore as believers, we must embrace the reality that Satan and his cohorts are very real enemies to everyone who accepts Jesus Christ as his or her personal Savior. The reason why is because Satan is angry that he no longer has dominion over us. According to Colossians 1:13 (AMP Version), "The Father has delivered and drawn us to Himself out of the control and the dominion of darkness and has transferred us into the kingdom of the Son of His love." Once believers are born again, we become part of a heavenly family, Godly kingdom, and are inducted into a spiritual army.

There have been several discussions about being a part of the heavenly family and books about the Godly kingdom, but what is lacking is why we are inducted into the spiritual army. The book of Revelation reveals that there was a war in heaven and Michael and his angels had to cast Satan and his cohorts out to the earth making hell their new home.

And there was war in heaven; Michael and his angels fought against the dragon; and the dragon fought and his angels. And prevailed not; neither was their place found any more in heaven. And the great dragon was cast out, that old serpent, called the devil, and Satan, which deceiveth the whole world: he was cast out into the earth, and his angels were cast out with him. And I heard a loud voice saying in heaven, now is come salvation, and strength, and the kingdom of our God, and the power of his Christ: for the accuser of our brethren is cast down, which accused them before our God day and night (Revelation 12:7-10).

Jesus stated that He "beheld Satan as lightning falling from heaven" (Luke 10:18). Satan was forced out of heaven to the earth realm and cannot return because he became uplifted in pride attempting to be God and he was brought down to the pit of hell (Isaiah 14:15). In doing so, he became the god of this world blinding the minds of everyone who does not believe in Jesus who is the Light and the image of God that would shine on them (2 Corinthians 4:4). According to 1 John 1:5, "God is Light and there is no darkness in Him at all." Therefore, every believer born of Jesus is now a part of the kingdom of Light (Ephesians 5:8). Likewise,

Satan and his cohorts are of the kingdom of darkness and everyone who does not accept Jesus lives and walks in that darkness. Because of this comparison of Light and darkness, every believer will encounter spiritual warfare each time Jesus exposes the darkness of Satan in a person or an atmosphere.

Even though the warfare begins when believers receive Jesus, it does not become intensified until we understand our authority. Jesus states, "Behold I give unto you power to tread on serpents and scorpions, and over all the power of the enemy; and nothing shall by any means hurt you" (Luke 10:19). The power that Jesus is referring to is the baptism of His Holy Spirit (Luke 24:49, Acts 1:8, 2). Why do we need this power? The warfare is real as well as the demonic spirits and Satan's weapons are "flaming missiles" aimed to destroy believers.

It is true that Jesus does not want us to praise Satan or blame him for every wrong occurrence in our lives; however, He also does not want us to be afraid to exercise our authority over and against activities that Satan employs to affect our lives. How can we walk in the authority if we do not acknowledge that Satan is a real enemy? It is a fact that Jesus has defeated Satan. Through His death, burial, and resurrection, Jesus received victory over sin, death, and the grave. As believers, we must accept and understand the impact of this truth for successful operation in spiritual warfare. Colossians 2:15, 2 Timothy 1:10, 1 Corinthians 15:54b (AMP Version), 1 Corinthians 15:55 and Hebrews 2:14 (KJV) renders support to the facts presented regarding Jesus' triumph over Satan.

> *God disarmed the principalities and powers that were ranged against us and made a bold display and public example of them, in triumphing over them in Him and in it (the cross) (Colossians 2:15).*

> *It is that purpose and grace which He now has made known and has fully disclosed and make real to us through the appearing of our Savior Christ Jesus, Who annulled death and made it of no effect and brought life and immortality (immunity from eternal death) to light through the Gospel (2 Timothy 1:10).*

> *Death is swallowed up utterly vanquished forever in and unto victory (1 Corinthians 15:54b).*

O death, where is thy sting? O grave, where is thy victory? (1 Corinthians 15:55).

Forasmuch then as the children are partakers of flesh and blood, he also himself likewise took part of the same; that through death he might destroy him that had the power of death, that is, the devil (Hebrews 2:14).

The aforementioned Scriptures make believers aware that Jesus did a complete work of destroying Satan and his works taking complete authority over him. Therefore, it is an extreme necessity that believers acknowledge the completed work of Jesus. By acknowledging what Jesus has already done, it empowers believers to stand triumphantly operating in authority over Satan with confidence because Jesus lives within us. Therefore, when Satan sees a believer walking in authority, he sees the Jesus within that person and is reminded of how Jesus openly defeated him!

To further empower us to confidently exercise our authority, Jesus informs us that He has the keys of hell and death (Revelation 1:18).

Reminding us of His authority, benefits all believers. While His Spirit dwells within our hearts, Jesus is at the right hand of God in heavenly places over all principalities, power, might, dominion, and every name that is named in this world and the one to come having all things under His feet and given the authority over all things to the church (Ephesians 1:20-22).

In other words, Jesus has all power and authority functioning in/through Him and all other supernatural powers are subject to Him (1 Peter 3:22). Why is this important? Knowing the authority and power that Jesus walks in is important because He gave those who believe in Him the same power. If Jesus who is the source of the believer's authority and power has victory over Satan and his cohorts, believers through Him have victory over Satan and his cohorts.

The problem is that many believers do not understand that we have the victory because we are being taught that Satan is not a threat and attempt to fight a spiritual war with fleshly weapons. As a result, many believers walk in spiritual defeat. Why should believers live defeated lives when we can be taught how to war? As a warrior God who is mighty in battle, God the Father teaches our hands to war and makes us skilled in warfare (Exodus 15:3, Psalms 18:34, 24:8).

Jesus knows how the spirit realm operates. He exposes the tactics of our enemy by taking our focus off the fleshly battle causing us to see into the spirit realm discerning the real warfare. What do we see? Satan and his cohorts are destined to hell forever. Due to this fact, the kingdom of darkness that he controls is trying to "seize upon and devour" as many people as he can by appearing as an angel of light or nonthreatening to capture souls that were never destined to join him in hell. Hence, when believers wrestle or contend, we simply remind Satan and his cohorts that they are defeated and have no authority over us or anything connected to us.

Just like the natural military, believers applying spiritual warfare attack Satan's chain of command by land, air, and sea. Paul explains that we do not wrestle against flesh and blood, but against principalities, powers, rulers of darkness of this world, and spiritual wickedness in high places (Ephesians 6:12). Whereas the natural military wars with guns, grenades, bombs, etc. to fight natural enemies, believers have to use spiritual weapons to fight spiritual enemies. Paul emphasizes that our weapons are not simply human or physical weapons, but they are mighty through God for the destruction and overthrow of the strongholds of Satan.

What are the mighty weapons that every believer must skillfully apply in warfare? They are the weapons of prayer, the Word of God, the name of Jesus, the Blood, praise, fasting, love, and forgiveness. If applied properly, each one of these weapons will assist spirit-filled believers in maintaining the victory Jesus gave us for our individual lives as well as overthrow the strongholds in someone else's life or atmosphere for the kingdom of God.

Introduction Review

1. What is the definition of warfare?

   _____

   _____

2. Do believers have an enemy? If so, who is it?

   _____

3. Who is the believers' Chain of Command and what is His function?

   _____

   _____

4. Why is Satan a real enemy?

   _____

   _____

5. Why are we inducted into a spiritual army?

   _____

   _____

6. Why is operating in your power as a believer important?

   _____

   _____

Weapons for Spiritual Warfare

7. What type of authority does Jesus have?

_____

_____

8. According to Luke 10:19, as believers, what type authority did Jesus give unto us?

_____

_____

_____

9. What is seen in the spirit realm?

_____

10. Name the 8 weapons for spiritual warfare.

   1.

   2.

   3.

   4.

   5.

   6.

   7.

   8.

Chapter One

The Weapon of Prayer

If thy people go out to battle against their enemy, whithersoever thou shalt send them, and shall pray unto the Lord toward the city which thou hast chosen, and toward the house that I have built for thy name; then hear thou in heaven their prayer and their supplication, and maintain their cause (1 Kings 8:44-45).

Prayer is a foundational principle in spiritual warfare. Equally as we need God to breathe His breath into us to live this natural life, we need prayer for our spiritual life. Prayer is so important that the disciples made a special request for Jesus to teach them how to pray (Luke 11:1). What is prayer? Prayer is communing with or having a conversation with God. The term conversation is applied here because God really talks back to us either through His Word or by the inner witness of His Spirit. Sometimes as believers we make it more difficult than it needs to be and miss the opportunity to have a great conversation with God. How often should believers pray? Jesus taught in Luke 18:1 that "men ought always to pray and not to faint." The reason why Jesus wants us to always pray is because without prayer and the Word believers will become weak living in our flesh.

As I stated in the previous chapter, we cannot perform spiritual warfare in our flesh. In ongoing warfare, prayer is essential (Ephesians 6:18, The Message Bible). Without perseverance in consistent prayer, believers will live defeated spiritual lives. However, believers who continue in intense prayer "makes tremendous power available that is dynamic in its working" (James 5:16, AMP Version). In addition, believers in warfare are alert watching in prayer and interceding on the behalf of the saints (Ephesians 6:18, AMP Version). Therefore, Satan constantly war against the prayer lives of the believers. While the believer may not understand, Satan understands prayer is an arsenal against the kingdom of darkness.

When King Solomon prayed the opening Scripture as part of his dedication to God for a new temple, it was profound. He interceded for Israel for the time of battle. Not only did he ask for divine protection, but he encouraged Israel to employ prayer as an integral weapon against the enemies present and future. In the same manner as prayer was employed by Israel in battle, believers should also employ this principle of prayer in our daily lives and spiritual warfare. Paul encouraged believers to always pray in the Spirit watching with perseverance (Ephesians 6:18). What he meant regarding perseverance in that Scripture text is "pray at all times, every occasion, and every season" (AMP Version).

Through prayer, our ears become fine tuned to the voice of God. Furthermore, believers enter into the spirit realm gaining power and favor with God while destroying Satan's kingdom. What do I mean when I say favor and power with God? Favor is God's unmerited grace extended to us whereby He attends to our prayers and answers them. This type of prayer is what the Apostle John considers a confident prayer (1 John 5:14-15). Along with favor, power is the ground that believers gain in the heavenly realm availing us to walk in the authority God gave us through Jesus Christ.

As we watch in prayer, God reveals plans for the lives of believers, their nation, and the kingdom of God. In addition, God exposes the plans of the enemy allowing believers to strategize and maintain victory in the midst of battles warring in prayer and taking back territory that belongs to them and God.

The Word of God reveals how the weapon of prayer was skillfully applied in warfare for men like Joshua, Elijah, and Hezekiah causing them to miraculously win battles. The Word of God also reveals how the weapon of intercessory prayer gave Daniel spiritual revelation and understanding for a nation, Peter a get out of jail free card, and cancels every assignment the enemy attempts to plot against the lives of believers.

Prayer is the weapon that called the elements to attention in the midst of the battle.

In the lives of Joshua and Elisha, God revealed how believers who have power and favor with Him in prayer can call the elements to obedience in battle. In the book of Joshua chapter ten, the Amorite nations came together to fight against Gibeon because they were at peace with Joshua and the Israelites. The Bible shares how Gibeon asked Joshua for assistance to war against the five Amorite kings and God said to Joshua, "Fear them not: for I have delivered them into thine hand; there shall not a man of them stand before thee" (v. 8). Why would God speak to Joshua before he went into battle about victory over the enemies?

Joshua 10:12-14 reveals that Joshua was a person of prayer who had power and favor with God.

> *Then spake Joshua to the Lord in the day when the Lord delivered up the Amorites before the children of Israel, and he said in the sight of Israel, Sun, stand thou still upon Gibeon; and thou, Moon, in the valley of Ajalon. And the sun stood still, and the moon stayed, until the people had avenged themselves upon their enemies. Is not this written in the book of Jasher? So the sun stood still in the midst of heaven, and hasted not to go down about a whole day. And there was no day like that before it or after it, that the Lord hearkened unto the voice of a man: for the Lord fought for Israel.*

Praise God! In the midst of the battle, Joshua took authority over the atmospheric elements in prayer commanding the sun and the moon to shine light on the enemy rendering total victory as God had promised. Joshua's enemies were many and great, but the power of prayer in the midst of his battle was greater. Even as Joshua took authority over his atmosphere through prayer, God has given believers the power to do the same operation in prayer.

Believers that employ the weapon of prayer in spiritual warfare trump the darkness of Satan. Without prayer, there is no level playing field or fair fight against spiritual enemies in our flesh. Why? We cannot fight in the natural spiritual beings we cannot see. However, prayer renders a level playing field for believers. When Satan gathers his cohorts to surround believers as the nations did Gibeon and Israel, prayer will cause the light of Jesus to shine exposing all the schemes of darkness arising against us. As a result, we will obtain the promised victory and gain the advantage.

Another occurrence of prayer calling the elements to attention was in the life of Elijah the Prophet. In 1 Kings chapter eighteen, the Bible gives the full account of how through prayer Elijah proved that water can be swallowed up by fire and a man can take authority over the rain from heaven. What was the battle really about? The battle was against the spirit of idolatry infiltrating through the leader Ahab causing the nation of Israel to turn from God and believe the god Baal was their source. Baal worship was a direct attack from Satan because Baal promoted sexual perversion and the murder of children. Due to those horrific actions, Elijah confronts the Baal worshippers and King Ahab decreeing that there would be no rain in Israel as he turns the hearts of the people back to God.

As a one man army armed only with the arsenal of prayer, Elijah met four hundred and fifty prophets of Baal on Mount Carmel. After the Baal worshippers prayed to their idol god Baal who could not hear, see, or show power, Elijah called the children of Israel to bear witness to trusting Yahweh God. He also demonstrated why it was vital to maintain power in prayer to/with the Living God.

First, Elijah built an altar to the Living God using twelve stones that represented the tribes of Israel circled by a trench. Second, he placed wood on the altar for the sacrifice, which is the normal routine for preparing a sacrifice to God. However, what Elijah did next was an attention getter in the sight of Israel. He instructed that the trench around the altar be filled with water that overflowed over the wood prepared for the sacrifice. 1 Kings 18:36-39 unfolds Elijah's plan of action.

And it came to pass at the time of the offering of the evening sacrifice, that Elijah the prophet came near, and said, Lord God of Abraham, Isaac, and of Israel, let it be known this day that thou art God in Israel, and that I am thy servant, and that I have done all these things at thy word (36).

Hear me, O Lord, hear me, that this people may know that thou art the Lord God, and that thou hast turned their heart back again (37).

Then the fire of the Lord fell, and consumed the burnt sacrifice, and the wood, and the stones, and the dust, and LICKED UP THE WATER THAT WAS IN THE TRENCH (38) (capitalized for emphasis).

And when the people saw it, THEY FELL on THEIR FACES: and THEY SAID, THE LORD, HE is the GOD; THE LORD, HE is the GOD (39) (capitalized for emphasis).

The natural course pertaining to water and fire is that water puts out fire. However, in this Scripture context, God answered Elijah's prayer as a consuming fire that "licked up the water" (Hebrews 12:29). Why was this important for the battle at hand? This was important for the children of

Israel to see and know that God is God and not Baal as well as to know that Elijah had power with God as His Prophet.

Furthermore, Elijah continued to show that he was skilled in the weapon of prayer as he prayed and the heavens yielded rain. 1 Kings 18:41 states, "And Elijah said unto Ahab, Get thee up, eat and drink; for there is a sound of abundance of rain." Directly after, there "was a great rain" (1 Kings 18:45). One would think from this demonstration that Elijah was a supernatural being. However, the book of James referring to 1 Kings 17:1 and 1 Kings 18:42-45 makes us aware that it was quite the opposite.

Elijah was a human being with a nature such as we have with feelings, affections, and a constitution like ours; and he prayed earnestly for it not to rain, and no rain fell on the earth for three years and six months. And, then, he prayed again and the heavens supplied rain and the land produced its crops as usual (James 5: 17-18, AMP Version).

The Apostle James lets us know Elijah was just a man who had power and favor in prayer. He prayed earnestly.[3] In other words, he prayed seriously, soberly, and sincerely in faith whereby making his prayer effective and "availing much." Elijah was a great Prophet of God operating in the same principle of prayer given to believers today that anything we ask believing and doubting not, God will do it! (Mark 11:23-24).

Another principle employed by Elijah is the principle of binding and loosing. Jesus explains this principle in Matthew 18:18.

> *Truly I tell you, whatever you forbid and declare to be improper and unlawful on earth must be what is already forbidden in heaven and whatever you permit and declare proper and lawful on the earth must be what is already permitted in heaven (AMP Version).*

Elijah's warfare in the spirit was great and intense; therefore, his operation of authority in the spirit realm had to be greater. Remember, Elijah was a "man" who had faith that his prayer was being heard by a great God. With

---

[3] *Webster's New World Roget's A-Z Thesaurus LoveToKnow*, n.d., s.v. "earnestly," accessed July 9, 2011, http://www.yourdictionary.com/quotes/earnestly.

this belief, he commanded or "forbid and declared that it was unlawful" for rain to fall for three years and six months. Consequently, heaven agreed with Elijah's decision and withheld the rain until Elijah permitted rain to be released at the appointed time. Why did God allow Elijah to use the weapon of prayer to forbid specifically rain? The idol gods Baal and Ashtoreth were considered to be gods of fertility to produce crops and rain.[4]

In order to prove that Baal and Ashtoreth were idols with no power or authority to produce the rain that God created, God chastened the entire nation to prove that He alone was God and there is none other. God assigned the task to Elijah to speak to Ahab and declare there will be no rain binding what was attributed to Baal to release the people of God from idolatry. Elijah was equipped with power and favor in prayer to command rain to be released and heaven permitted rain to win the hearts of a people and bring restoration to a nation. What is fascinating about how Elijah functioned in the weapon of prayer is he did not have the information that believers have today regarding the principle of binding and loosing.

[4.] Merrill F. Unger. *Unger's Bible Dictionary* (Chicago: Moody Press, 1977), 412-413, s.v., "Ashtoreth and Baal."

However, he functioned in the principle with great assurance defeating the enemy.

Even as Elijah operated in the principle of binding and loosing or permitting and releasing, believers must do the same. Believers operate in this power by the Holy Spirit. The Holy Spirit assists each one who allows him/her in prayer with great power to speak to the elements even as Joshua and Elijah. Jesus gave every believer authority and power to bind every attack of Satan and loose what God instructs with the full backing of heaven to destroy the works of Satan against our individual lives and the kingdom of God.

An example of the principle of binding and loosing the spirits of idolatry, the antichrist, and the influences of darkness in an atmosphere during prayer for spiritual warfare may be applied as follows:

In prayer state, "Satan in the name of Jesus I bind the spirits of idolatry, the antichrist, and the power of the influences of darkness and send them to the pit of hell from which they have come. In the name of Jesus, I loose the Spirit of Truth, the light of Jesus to shine in every dark place, and His salvation against these demonic forces. I bind and take authority over every demonic activity in the atmosphere and forbid your operation in the name of Jesus and send you and your cohorts to the pit of hell. In the name of Jesus, I permit and loose God's delivering power and presence against Satan's forces and I plea the blood of Jesus against Satan's works, activities, and his cohorts. The blood of Jesus prevails against you!

Prayer is the weapon that caused Hezekiah to cancel the assignment of the enemy.

Similar to Joshua and Elijah, Hezekiah applied the weapon of prayer to cancel the assignment of the enemy. In Isaiah chapters 36-37, the author describes how king Sennacherib of Assyrian attempted to intimidate King Hezekiah and Israel to surrender and serve Assyria. Sennacherib sent his military captain Rabshakeh to do the job for Assyria. The spiritual warfare tactic was psychological warfare. In Isaiah 36:2a, 4, 13-18 (AMP Version), Rabshakeh attempted to convince Israel not to trust in Hezekiah as a leader or trust in God.

And the king of Assyria sent Rabshakeh (the military official) from Lacish (the Judean fortress commanding the road from Egypt) to King Hezekiah at Jerusalem with a great army (2a). And the Rabshakeh said to them, Say to Hezekiah, Thus says the great king, the king of Assyria; What reason for confidence is this in which you trust? (4).

Then the Rabshakeh stood and cried with a loud voice in the language of the Jews; Hear the words of the great king, the king of Assyria! Thus says the king: Let not Hezekiah deceive you, for he will not be able to deliver you (13-14).

Nor let Hezekiah make you trust in and rely on the Lord, saying, The Lord will surely deliver us; this city will not be delivered into the hand of the king of Assyria (15).

Do not listen to Hezekiah, for thus says the king of Assyria: Make your peace with me and come out to me; and eat every one from his own vine and every one from his own fig tree and drink every one the water of his own cistern, until I come and take you away to a land like your own land, a land of grain and wine, a land of bread and vineyards (16-17).

> *Beware lest Hezekiah persuade and mislead you by saying, The Lord will deliver us. Has anyone of the gods of the nations ever delivered his land out of the hand of the king of Assyria? (18)*

In reading the Scripture text, it is evident that Rabshakeh operated skillfully in his weapon of choice for warfare against the nation of Israel. What was Rabshakeh's weapon of choice? His weapon of choice was the weapon of spoken words to minister to Israel's mind. What did Rabshakeh say? In his boast about the power of Assyria, Rabshakeh details how Assyria had defeated other nations with their great and powerful army. While the Assyrian army surrounded Israel, Rabshakeh declared with confidence Assyria would surely destroy King Hezekiah and Israel regardless of their God. By the display of the Assyrian army and the boldness of Rabshakeh speaking, Assyria attempted to psychologically cripple and paralyze Israel with fear.

With this method of warfare applied towards Israel, the Assyrian army assumed that without physically touching Israel, Israel would simply give themselves and their inheritance over to Assyria. In turn, Assyria promised to bless Israel in another land with the things God had already given them. It appeared that Hezekiah and Israel were bullied into a corner; however, Rabshakeh boldly made a challenge to Hezekiah and his God. Also, what Rabshakeh did not understand was that he fought kings that served idol gods instead of a king who served the Living God!

In response, Hezekiah employed the weapon of prayer. In one instance Hezekiah relied on the prayer of Isaiah the Prophet to pray and intercede for the nation. In another instance, he prayed directly to the Lord for himself.

Looking at the first instance, Hezekiah and the nation were weakened by the words spoken and needed assistance from someone who had direct communication with God and was a skilled warrior in prayer. This person was Isaiah the Prophet. Hezekiah sent Eliakim, Shebna, and the elders of the priest to Isaiah with a message to pray. Isaiah 37:3-4, 6-8 (AMP Version), reveals that the Prophet Isaiah rendered a response to King Hezekiah from God.

And they said to him (Isaiah), Thus says Hezekiah: This day is a day of trouble and distress and of rebuke and of disgrace; for children have come to the birth, and there is no strength to bring them forth (3).

It may be that the Lord your God will hear the words of Rabshakeh, whom the king of Assyria, his master has sent to mock, reproach, insult, and defy the living God, and will rebuke the words which the Lord your God has heard. Therefore lift up your prayer for the remnant (of His people) that is left (4).

And Isaiah said to them, You shall say to your master, Thus says the Lord: Do not be afraid because of the words which you have heard, with which the servants of the king of Assyria have reviled and blasphemed Me (6).

Behold, I will put a spirit in him so that he will hear a rumor and return to his own land, and I will cause him to fall by the sword of his own land (7).

> *So the Rabshakeh returned and found the king of Assyria fighting against Libnah {a fortified city of Judah}; for he had heard that the king had departed from Lachish (8).*

According to aforementioned text, God assured Hezekiah that Israel does not have to "be AFRAID because of the WORDS which you have heard" because Rabshakeh will return back to Assyria and "fall by the sword."

In the second instance, King Sennacherib sent WORDS to provoke fear and terror to King Hezekiah again, however, this time the WORDS were in writing or in the form of a letter.

> *And Hezekiah received the letter from the hand of messengers and read it. And Hezekiah went up to the house of the Lord and spread it before the Lord. And Hezekiah prayed to the Lord (Isaiah 37:14-15 AMP Version).*

Hezekiah employed the spiritual weapon of prayer because he knew prayer was effective for Israel. In addition, God took this interaction with the Assyrian king personal. God made it perfectly clear that by attacking Hezekiah and Israel, King Sennacherib and his Assyrian army was making a direct attack against Him. This meant God had to personally deal with this enemy for His people. Isaiah 37:33-38a (AMP Version) reveals this truth and benefit.

> *Therefore thus says the Lord concerning the king of Assyria: He shall not come into this city or shoot an arrow here or come before it with shield or cast up a siege mound against it (33).*
>
> *By the way he came, by the same way he shall return, and he shall not come into this city, says the Lord. For I will defend this city to save it, for My own sake and for the sake of My servant David (34-35).*
>
> *And the Angel of the Lord went forth, and slew 185,000 in the camp of the Assyrians; and when {the living} arose early in the morning, behold, all these were dead bodies (36).*
>
> *So Sennacherib king of Assyria departed and returned and dwelt at Nineveh. And as he was worshiping in the house of Nisroch his god, Adrammelech and Sharezer his sons killed him with the sword (37-38a).*

The WORDS that the Assyrian king attempted to instill in the minds of Israel were, "do not trust in Hezekiah or trust in God because Assyria was greater." Hezekiah displayed to the nation that the weapon of prayer is the only defense that they could trust when overwhelmed by the tactics of the enemy. Indeed, the spirit of fear and intimidation may have worked against the other nations who fought a spear and sword battle with Assyria. However, Hezekiah trusted God in prayer and God displayed to the nation that prayer works! God defended His nation and canceled the assignment of Assyria. By killing the soldiers, God proved that the Assyrian army was not as great as they presumed and Sennacherib's death guaranteed Israel would not see this enemy again.

Believers of God, we need to know that the same God that inclined to the prayer of Hezekiah will incline to our prayers in the midst of overwhelming circumstances. When Satan tries to intimidate believers psychologically with words of failure, discouragement, doubt and unbelief, or fear of trusting God in circumstances, we must employ the weapon of prayer. Someone may say, "I can't or I am too weak." Then do as Hezekiah did and call on someone who can intercede in prayer on your behalf. What is intercessory prayer pertaining to spiritual warfare? It is when believers or a believer stands in the gap and fights through prayer demonic influences or attacks on the behalf of others. God heard the prayer of the Prophet Isaiah on the behalf of Hezekiah and the prayer of Hezekiah on the behalf of Israel.

Begin to employ the weapon of prayer against the WORDS of Satan today by praying this simple prayer for yourself or on the behalf of someone else.

Satan, I cancel every verbal and written threat against me, my family, purpose, ministry, and destiny in the name of Jesus. Your WORDS do not prosper nor take root in me, but they will fall to the ground, they die, and do not come to pass in the name of Jesus. I send every assault back to the sender and their WORDS fall on their own heads. I plead the blood of Jesus against you (Satan) and your cohorts in the name of Jesus and His blood prevails! In the name of Jesus, I decree victory in this situation and circumstance for me and for those who I am interceding on their behalf. Amen.

Intercessory Prayer is the weapon that gave Peter a get out of jail free card and Daniel spiritual revelation and understanding for Israel.

In the same manner as Hezekiah, the weapon of prayer through intercession produced a great deliverance for the Apostle Peter:

Now about that time Herod the king stretched forth his hands to vex certain of the church. And he killed James the brother of John with the sword. And because he saw it pleased the Jews, he proceeded further to take Peter also. Then were the days of unleavened bread. And when he had apprehended him, he put him in prison, and delivered him to four quaternions of soldiers to keep him; intending after Easter to bring him forth to the people. Peter therefore was kept in prison: but prayer was made without ceasing of the church unto God for him (Acts 12:1-5).

During this time, the body of Christ was going through great persecution and the devil's instrument of destruction was King Herod. His assignment was to kill the church leaders. After he had successfully killed James, he took Peter and locked him up. The Bible states that the church had a prayer meeting and prayed for Peter "without ceasing." This is important.

Although Peter was a person of prayer, the agreement and intercession[5] of the prayers of others on his behalf canceled the assignment of death planned by Satan through Herod.

> *Again I tell you, if two of you on earth agree (harmonized together, make a symphony together) about whatever (anything and everything) they may ask, it will come to pass and be done for them by My Father in heaven (Matthew 18:19, AMP Version).*

While the saints were praying for Peter, there were supernatural manifestations taking place on his behalf. In prison, Peter was asleep, chained, and guarded by sixteen soldiers. However, God sent an angel who woke him up, broke his chains, opened the iron gates of the prison, and lead him out to safety. Peter thought he was having a vision of the things that were taking place. It was not until he had come out of the city that he realized God had delivered him from death. What is so amazing is Peter went to Mary's house where the saints were praying for him and knocked on the door.

---

[5] James Orr. *International Standard Bible Encyclopedia*, s.v. "intercession," accessed July 9, 2011, http://www.biblestudytools.com/encyclopedias/isbe/

And when he knocked at the gate of the porch, a maid named Rhoda came to answer. And recognizing Peter's voice, in her joy she failed to open the gate, but ran in and told the people that Peter was standing before the porch gate. They said to her, You are crazy! But she persistently and strongly and confidently affirmed that it was the truth. They said, It is his angel! But meanwhile Peter continued knocking, and when they opened the gate, and saw him, they were amazed (Acts 12:13-16, AMP Version).

What happened in this passage of Scripture is monumental. The saints of God were in constant prayer for Peter's deliverance; however, when God delivered him or answered their prayer manifesting Peter as evidence, they did not believe it was done.

Believers, it is important when interceding for others in spiritual warfare to know and recognize when God has answered the prayer. How will we know? The Holy Spirit will bear witness that we have availed in the spiritual intercession warfare yielding a release in our spirits. At this point, believers have the liberty to proclaim that God has done what we have prayed.

Even as Rhoda was sensitive to hear the knocking at the door recognizing it was Peter and was called crazy because she told the saints our answer is at the door, you as a believer may be called crazy because you proclaim victory despite of what it appears to be in the natural realm. Like Rhoda, you may be the only one with the revelation and a release in your spirit that the prayer of intercession has worked in the matters at hand. Do not allow the non-belief of others to confuse or deter you. If you hold fast to your confession of faith, God will reveal the manifested answered prayer to them too.

Another example of spiritual warfare in intercession is in the book of Daniel. In Daniel chapter ten, Daniel combined prayer with fasting to receive spiritual revelation from God regarding the nation of Israel's future. Although God heard his prayer the first day, Daniel had to wait twenty-one days to receive the answer because there was spiritual warfare taking place in the heavenly realm. Satan tried to hinder the answer, but the angel of God brought the answer.

Then said he unto me, Fear not, Daniel: for from the first day that thou didst set thine heart to understand and to chasten thyself before thy God, thy words were heard, and I am come for thy words. But the prince of the kingdom of Persia withstood me one and twenty days: but lo, Michael, one of the chief princes, came to help me; and I remained there with the kings of Persia. Now I am come to make thee understand what shall befall thy people in the latter days for yet the vision is for many days (Daniel 10:12-14).

In concurrence with Ephesians 6:12, Satan had spiritual wickedness in high places assigning a chief demon over the kingdom of Persia. This demon warred in the heavenly realm with an angel of God for twenty-one days with one goal. His goal was to keep Daniel from receiving the revelatory answer that would give understanding regarding the current state of Israel, the revelation of the purpose of Jesus, and God's plans for Israel's future. The warfare regarding Daniel's prayer was so intense that God had to send Michael (His chief angel) to fight against the chief demon of Persia to release the other angel to bring Daniel his answer. He encouraged Daniel that God heard him from the beginning and explained why there was a delay.

This passage of Scripture reveals three things to us as believers. The first thing is that spiritual warfare in the heavenly realm during prayer is very real to believers and spiritual beings such as angels and demons do exist. The second thing is that delays in our prayers to God may just be Satan trying to hinder the answer and does not mean that God did not hear the prayer, especially when believers are interceding for others. The third thing this passage reveals is that God will directly intervene and intercede on the behalf of believers against the attacks and schemes of the devil.

While waiting, believers warring in prayer may become weary and the devil will lie telling us that God did not hear our prayer or He is angry with us. Do not believe the lies of the devil. Even when we are weary, believers must trust God. In addition, we must receive the same assurance given to Daniel that God heard our prayer the "first day." Like Daniel, God will send ministering angels to strengthen and remind us that He is not angry; but, He loves us. For believers, God will give kingdom direction and revelation knowledge for the body of Christ in this last day.

As a result of the pending information believers may receive from God, our warfare in prayer may be intensified. However, the answer to our prayers is also just around the corner.

Chapter One Review

1. Why is prayer important?

   _____

   _____

   _____

2. For believers, what happens through prayer?

   _____

   _____

   _____

3. What does God reveal?

   _____

   _____

4. Can you take authority over your atmosphere?

   _____

5. What shines a light on the schemes of darkness?

   _____

6. How many false prophets were against one true prophet?

   _____

Weapons for Spiritual Warfare The Weapon of Prayer

7. What did Elijah do?

_____

_____

8. How did God answer Elijah's prayer?

_____

_____

9. Was Elijah a supernatural being?

_____

_____

10. What is the principle of binding and loosing?

_____

_____

_____

11. What did Elijah have to operate in prayer so intensely?

_____

_____

12. Who assists believers to bind and loose?

_____

13. What is psychological warfare?

14. What is the purpose of psychological warfare?

15. How did prayer cancel the assignment of Sennacherib?

16. What was the weapon used by the Assyrians?

17. The Assyrians used the aforementioned weapon to do what?

18. What is the first type of prayer Hezekiah applied?

Weapons for Spiritual Warfare The Weapon of Prayer

19. Satan uses words in two ways to provoke fear. What are they?

_____

_____

20. Who took this attack against Hezekiah personal?

_____

21. What were the WORDS the Assyrian king attempted to instill in Hezekiah?

_____

_____

22. What are some of the WORDS Satan may be trying to instill in your mind?

_____

_____

_____

23. What is intercessory prayer in spiritual warfare?

_____

_____

24. What did the church do for the Apostle Peter?

_____

25. If you are a person of prayer, can people pray for you?

26. What happens when we pray?

27. We must be sensitive to what?

28. When did God hear Daniel's prayer?

29. What could be a reason for a prayer delay?

30. What 3 things did God reveal to us through Daniel's prayer life?

Chapter Two

The Weapon of the Word

...and the sword of the Spirit, which is the Word of God (Ephesians 6:17b)
God's Word is an indispensable weapon (Ephesians 6:17b, Message Bible Version).

The Word of God is fundamental because it is the foundational weapon for every weapon employed in spiritual warfare. It is the scale for the lives of believers. Most of the time, we refer to the Bible as the Holy Scriptures or "the Word of God." What makes the Word of God so effective is the fact that It is Jesus Himself revealing Himself and the desire of the Father from eternity to/for the kingdom of God (John 1:1). He as the Word has standing power, never fails, and endures forever (1 Peter 1:24-25). From the beginning, the Word of God compels darkness to be dismissed facilitating Light to reign. To believers, Jesus the Word is the Living Water and Bread that nourishes life to the spirit man with resurrection and reconciliation power to heal, set free, and deliver. To Satan, the Word of God is a constant reminder of an open defeat by Jesus and the foretelling of his demise.

As believers embrace the relevance of the Word of God, the Holy Spirit gives instruction, direction, and revelation to function in the power of the Word. In spiritual warfare, the Word of God weapon is an indispensable Sword with dual capabilities written and spoken penetrating the spirit realm to simultaneously transform lives and demolish the kingdom of darkness.

Why describe the Word of God as Indispensable and a Sword?

The Word of God is described as "an indispensable weapon." The Merriam-Webster's Dictionary states that the word "indispensable" means absolutely necessary, essential, all-important, critical, imperative, integral, required, and a vital requisite.[6] Why is the Word indispensable? Addressing God's expectations for His Word in the lives of the children of Israel, Moses explains the Word's indispensability giving divine order for incorporation in our everyday lives:

> *And these words which I am commanding you this day shall be first in your own minds and hearts; then you shall whet and sharpen them so as*

---

[6] *Merriam-Webster's Collegiate Dictionary*, 11 ed. s.v., "indispensable," accessed May 16, 2012, http://www.merriam-webster.com.

> *to make them penetrate, and teach and impress them diligently upon the minds and hearts of your children, and shall talk of them when you sit in your house and when you walk by the way, and when you lie down and when you rise up. And you shall bind them as a sign upon your hand, and they shall be as frontlets (forehead bands) between your eyes. And you shall write them upon the doorposts of your house and on your gates (Deuteronomy 6:6-9 AMP Version).*

According to the text, God admonishes the children of Israel to first place the Word of God in their hearts. Then, God admonishes them to speak and teach the Word to their children, keep it before their eyes, and expose it openly in their homes. For the children of Israel, it is clear that the Word of God was imperative. In the same manner as the children of Israel, the Word of God is also imperative for believers.

Even as Israel was required to dwell in the Word in every aspect, believers must have Jesus the Living Word dwelling deep in our hearts (Colossians 3:16). When the Word dwells, it keeps our feet from slipping and believers from operating in sin (Psalms 37:31, 119:11). Moreover, as we meditate on the written Word every day, the Word of God becomes an integral part of our lives and language. Being skillful in the knowledge and application of the Word of God is a critical component for serious spiritual warfare. This goes beyond just quoting a Scripture reference. There must be an assurance in the application that the Word of God carries weight to do what is being quoted.

It is crucial to believe that the Word of God is alive to do serious damage to Satan's kingdom. For this reason Satan attempts to deceive many believers to approach the Bible (the Word of God) as an ordinary literary book. Satan originated lies that the Word of God is boring, difficult to understand, and should not be taken literal because a man wrote it anyway. For non-believers, Satan's words may be fact because the Gospel is hid to those who are lost (2 Corinthians 4:3).

However, it is quite the contrary for born again believers. Although the Bible has been on the best sellers list for a long period of time, it is not an ordinary novel inspired from human intellect. The words that are referred to as Scriptures or the Word of God are God-breathed.

Every Scripture is God-breathed (given by His inspiration) and profitable for instruction, for reproof and conviction of sin, for correction of error and discipline in obedience, and for training in righteousness (in holy living in conformity to God's will in thought, purpose, and action) (2 Timothy 3:16, AMP Version).

Furthermore, the Word of God is not willed by human interpretation, but by the Holy Spirit's guidance.

Yet first you must understand this, that no prophecy of Scripture is a matter of any personal or private or special interpretation (loosening, solving). For no prophecy ever originated because some man willed it (to do so it never came by human impulse), but men spoke from God who were borne along (moved and impelled) by the Holy Spirit. (2 Peter 1:20-21, AMP Version)

Why is it important in spiritual warfare to know how the Word originated? It is important because no human soul exists without God's breath and God is Spirit and Truth. Knowing that God breathed breath into humankind making us living souls gives credence to how powerful

His breath constructs life in the Word. Even as natural breath has movement in our bodies, the Word of God has movement in the spiritual realm making it an indispensable weapon against the movement of darkness. Anything produced by supernatural life and breath cannot possibly be boring. The life of the Word moves in truth exposing the lies of Satan.

Satan makes the implication of boredom because the Holy Spirit has an assignment in the Word against him and the kingdom of darkness. Satan wants believers to be ignorant of our purpose and power only given by the Word of God. The Word teaches believers the right way to live, convicts and corrects us when we are not meeting that standard of holy living, and reveals the will of God for our lives. It also teaches believers who Satan is, his nature, and exposes the truth of his defeat by Jesus. In addition, the Word reveals how through Jesus believers have victory over Satan and his cohorts. Satan recognizes the authority of the Word of God because the Word has been there from the beginning. He also knows the Word is God and testifies of Jesus (John 1:1, 5:39). For this purpose believers cannot approach the Word of God with an attitude of boredom.

Believers have to approach the Word of God enthusiastically understanding it is our lifeline (John 6:51). Believers must find joy in consuming the Word of God remembering it is a mighty weapon. If believers lack understanding of the necessity of our Word weapon, we are at a disadvantage in our spiritual warfare walking in defeat instead of maintaining the victory Jesus already gave to the believer. Conversely, believers who have knowledge and understanding are not afraid to engage in warfare applying the Word skillfully.

Any believer lacking this understanding, the good news is all we have to do is ask for understanding. 2 Timothy 2:7 encourages believers to, "Think over these things I am saying understand them and grasp their application for the Lord will grant you full insight and understanding in everything" (AMP Version). The best person to ask for understanding of the Word is the person who wrote the book, God. His Holy Spirit moved on the holy men of God by His inspiration. The Holy Spirit makes the Word come to life and assists us with the revelation and understanding we need.

When Satan tells you as a believer that you cannot read the Word because it is too hard to understand, pray and ask God to reveal by His Holy Spirit greater knowledge, wisdom, and understanding of the Word. The Apostle Paul prayed this prayer for the believers:

> *That the God of our Lord Jesus Christ, the Father of glory, may give unto you the spirit of wisdom and revelation in the knowledge of Him: The eyes of your understanding being enlightened; that ye may know what is the hope of his calling, and what the riches of the glory of his inheritance in the saints (Ephesians 1:17-18).*

Ask God to open your eyes to see the wondrous things in the Word and hide every word in your heart that you will not sin against him availing a free flow of the Word from a pure heart (Psalm 119:11, 18). Pray that every Word will be sown so deep in the ground of your heart that you will do the Word and not just hear it (James 1:22). Timothy encourages believers that we become skillful in the Word of God by experience with the Word.

> *Study and be eager and do your utmost to present yourself to God approved (tested by trial), a workman who has no cause to be ashamed, correctly analyzing and accurately dividing (rightly handling and skillfully teaching) the Word of Truth (2 Timothy 2:15, AMP Version).*

Finally, pray that God will help make the Word relevant in your life, the lives of others, and in spiritual warfare.

The Word weapon identified as the Sword of the Spirit

The Word of God does not end with the description of an indispensable weapon, but the weapon is identified as the Sword of the Spirit. A sword is a weapon having a long straight or curved blade sharp-edged on one or both sides with one end pointed and the other fixed in a handle. This weapon is a symbol of military power in war causing death, destruction, slaughter, and violence.[7] Based on the definition, it is evident that a natural sword used properly causes severe damage or death to an enemy.

---

[7] *Dictionary.com Unabridged Random House Inc.* s.v., "sword," accessed April 28, 2012, http:// dictionary.reference.com/browse/sword.

In comparison to a natural sword, the Word of God as the Sword of the Spirit is sharper than the natural two-edged sword. The Word has greater capabilities supernaturally to do greater damage to the kingdom of darkness. Having a dual function spoken and written, the Word of God as a double-edged sword in the hands of skilled believers proclaims the truth of what is written.

> *For the Word that God speaks is alive and full of power making it active, operative, energizing, and effective; it is sharper than any two-edged sword, penetrating to the dividing line of the breath of life (soul) and the immortal spirit and of joints and marrow of the deepest part of our nature, exposing and sifting and analyzing and judging the very thoughts and purposes of the heart (Hebrews 4:12, AMP Version).*

Why is the Sword of the Word considered so powerful? It is powerful because the Word of God is alive and active penetrating the deepest parts of natural man, drawing the dividing line of soul and spirit, and leads us to the saving knowledge of Jesus as the Christ. At the same time, the Word of God penetrates between mortal, immortal, natural, and supernatural exposing the unseen works of Satan and his cohorts to the believers. Just like a natural sword, the Sword of the Word of God in warfare cuts asunder the stratagems of Satan in every direction bringing into play the tremendous harmony of the spoken and the written Word.

The Spoken Word in Spiritual Warfare

Through the Sword of the Spirit, God spoke everything into existence. Genesis chapter one states over and over again that "God said, called, and saw." Directly after God speaks, what He says manifests. When the spoken Word of God has an assignment to fulfill, the assignment is accomplished producing an effect. Regardless of what is manifesting as reality in the natural realm, the Word has an assignment and is equipped to destroy the powers of darkness in every level of the stratosphere.

> *For as the rain and snow come down from the heavens, and return not there again, but water the earth and make it bring forth and sprout, that it may give seed to the sower and bread to the eater. So shall my Word be that goes forth out of My mouth: it shall not return to Me void (without producing any effect, useless), but it shall accomplish that which*

I please and purpose and it shall prosper in the thing for which I sent It (Isaiah 55:10-11, AMP Version).

He sends forth His commandment to the earth; His word runs very swiftly (Psalm 147:15, AMP Version).

Then said the Lord to me, You have seen well, for I am alert and active, watching over My word to perform it (Jeremiah 1:12, AMP Version).

As Spirit-filled believers, God has given us the same authority to employ the Sword of the Spirit to speak things into existence and dismiss the influences of the kingdom of darkness. In addition, the Holy Spirit gives power to our tongue to speak life or death in spiritual combat against Satan's tactics (Proverbs 18:21). There is an answer in the Word of God for any and every situation of attack. For that reason, believers must know the written Word because we can only speak what we know is written. When we know the right Scripture to speak and send, we will see the manifested results.

When Satan attempts to render a demonic attack to arrest the bodies, minds, families, finances, and spirits of believers, the weapon of the Word of God must be spoken and sent to cancel the assignment. How is this done? First, combine the weapon of prayer with the Word to bind the spirit Satan has assigned. Then, send a direct counter attack by proclaiming the Word of God.

Some believers think that sickness is part of life, having financial struggles is the will of God, being depressed is just a medical situation, and a family member's destructive behavior is how he or she will remain. Those are all lies from the devil. The devil does not want believers prevailing in the spoken Word because it works against every demonic assignment. Remember, God's Word runs quickly, is active, and He Himself is watching over It to do what is being spoken.

The Spoken Word against the Spirit of Infirmity

For instance, there is a spoken Word of God that addresses spirits of infirmity, lack, and bondage. If sickness and disease have attacked the bodies of believers or their families, the Word of God calls this a spirit of infirmity. In the Word, Jesus declares He has healed all sickness and disease whether physically, emotionally, or mentally (Matthew 4:23). Therefore, believers must speak the Word in the atmosphere regardless of how it appears. Begin to speak by the power of the Holy Spirit and send the Sword of the Word on assignment to destroy the spirit of infirmity. Remember, the Sword of the Spirit understands spoken direction and it will go and not return void. Therefore, speak to the spirit of infirmity and remind Satan that the plagues of Egypt (the World) are not for the obedient believers of God.

> *Saying, If you will diligently hearken to the voice of the Lord your God and will do what is right in His sight, and will listen to and obey His commandments and keep all His statutes,* ***I will put none of the diseases upon you*** *which I brought upon the Egyptians,* ***for I am the Lord Who heals you*** *(Exodus 15:26, AMP Version).*

Remind Satan that Jesus covered your healing, the healing of your loved ones, and those you are interceding for in prayer on the cross.

> *But he (Jesus) was wounded for our transgressions, he was bruised for our iniquities: the chastisement of our peace was upon him; and* ***with his stripes we are healed*** *(Isaiah 53:5).*

Peter speaking what Isaiah had spoken stated, ***"by whose stripes ye were healed"*** *(1 Peter 2:24).*

..they brought Him all who were sick, those afflicted with various diseases and torments, those under the power of demons, and epileptics, and paralyzed people, and ***He healed them*** *(Matthew 4:24, AMP Version).*

The Lord ***heals all your diseases*** *(Psalm 103:3).*

When even was come they brought unto him many that were possessed with devils and ***he cast out the spirits with his word, and healed all that were sick*** *(Matthew 8:16).*

And thus He fulfilled what was spoken by the prophet Isaiah, He Himself took (in order to carry away) ***our weaknesses and infirmities and bore away our diseases*** *(Matthew 8:17, AMP Version).*

If someone is sick or near death in their home, church, hospital, or a loved one is on a destructive pattern, believers have faith and send the Word of

God. Psalm 107:20 (AMP Version) reminds us that, "He sends forth His word and heals them and rescues them from the pit and destruction."

When a woman of God was sick eighteen years and the centurion's servant was near death, Jesus spoke and sent His Word on assignment. The book of Luke gives an account of how the Word worked for both the centurion's servant and the woman. Let us look at how the Word was assigned to the centurion servant's life:

> *Now a centurion had a bond servant who was held in honor and highly valued by him, who was sick and at the point of death. And when the centurion heard of Jesus, he sent some Jewish elders to Him, requesting Him to come and make his bond servant well. And Jesus went with them. But when He was not far from the house, the centurion sent some friends to Him, saying, Lord, do not trouble Yourself for I am not sufficiently worthy to have You come under my roof; Neither did I consider myself worthy to come to You. But just speak a word, and my servant boy will be healed. And when the messengers who had been sent returned to the house, they found the bond servant, who had been ill quite well again (Luke 7:2-3, 6-7, 10 AMP Version).*

The Word of God completed the assignment! What is so fascinating about the Word of God's movement in the centurion's servant life is the centurion's perspective to the Word. He considered himself and his house unworthy to come before the presence of Jesus the Living Word; yet, he had faith to believe that when the Living Word speaks, it has the power to produce results. Send the Word on assignment and allow God to be accountable for fulfilling the results.

Although it is true that Jesus always healed everyone who believed He could heal them, He also was moved with compassion to heal when He discerned the spirit of infirmity in operation in a life. This is evident as Jesus speaks to a woman of God bound by the spirit of infirmity for eighteen years attending church.

And there was a woman there who for eighteen years had had an infirmity caused by a spirit (a demon of sickness). She was bent completely forward and utterly unable to straighten herself up or to look upward. And when Jesus saw her, He called her to Him and said to her, Woman, you are released from your infirmity! Then He laid His

> *hands on her, and instantly she was made straight, and she recognized and thanked and praised God (Luke 13: 11-13, AMP Version).*

The text reveals that the Word Himself took notice of a woman in the midst of a worship service. Jesus knew she had eighteen years of bondage, but she remained faithful to the house of God where the Word was being preached. Naturally, she appeared crippled because of the physical manifestations of the demonic activity of the spirit of infirmity. This natural appearance limited the woman's movement and function where she could not look up. Jesus, the Word, had to speak to her spirit because it is the place where worship takes place. He took authority over every emotion of hopelessness, unbelief, and unworthiness and literally brought her to Himself in a higher place of faith and hope. Despite the eighteen year hold that the spirit of infirmity obtained, the spoken Word grabbed her total attention long enough for Jesus to proclaim, "Woman, you are released from your infirmity!"

Notice that Jesus said, "Your infirmity." Believers, we do not have to receive the spirit of infirmity. Once sickness and disease is received by a person, the person takes ownership of the fruit the spirit of infirmity attempts to produce within him/her. Do not consent to the perspective that sickness is the will of God for your life, or I am unworthy to be healed, or I have been going through this so long and there is no hope. Be confident that the Sword of the spoken Word penetrates against the spirit of infirmity regardless how long it has lingered. Even when you may have given up hope or limitations appear, stay in the midst of worship where the Word is being spoken. Remember, the spoken Word of God is alive and active. The Word of God is not subject to our projected perspective of limitations or unworthiness. Jesus still heals! Speak the Word of God because there is power in the spoken Word to perform a complete work.

The Spoken Word against the Spirits of Lack and Bondage

In the same manner as the Word penetrates against the spirit of infirmity, it also penetrates against spirits of lack and bondage. While it may be true that most believers have experienced lack, we must acknowledge that lack is a spiritual enemy. Whether the need is financial, emotional, or spiritual, it is the spirit of lack. The Apostle John reveals that God's desire is for the believer to have a prosperous life (3 John 1:2).

Despite what Satan illustrates in the situation, God does not desire believers to lack in any aspect. Therefore, in the situations where lack attempts to reign, believers must employ the Sword of the spoken Word for application.

Psalm 23:1-3 and Philippians 4:19 are powerful assaults against the spirit of lack because both Scriptures assure believers that the Father will provide in every aspect of our lives. David speaks of God's provision as our Shepherd renewing our spirits and giving direction:

> *The Lord is my Shepherd (to feed, guide, and shield me), I shall not lack. He makes me lie down in fresh tender green pastures; He leads me beside the still and restful waters. He refreshes and restores my life, (my self); He leads me in the paths of righteousness (uprightness and right standing with Him–not for my earning it, but) for His name's sake (Psalm 23:1-3, AMP Version).*

The Apostle Paul attests that through Jesus every need is met:

> *And my God will liberally supply (fill to the full) your every need according to His riches in glory in Christ Jesus (Philippians 4:19, AMP Version).*

Bondage

Like lack, the same is true for bondage. Bondage of any sort is a spirit. With the spirit of bondage, comes fear and destruction. Satan desires to enslave believers or their families. There are so many believers bound to habits, relationships, and situations that Jesus has already spoken by His Word freedom. Furthermore, Satan tells the believer that what he/she is bound to is his/her private struggle which is an excuse allotting the influence of the power of darkness to reign in the situation with torment and fear. Satan also insists that the loved ones of the believers will never break free from the bondage of sin, addiction, or destruction, nor become saved or delivered. Let me reiterate, Satan is a liar! Trust Jesus for your freedom and the freedom of your loved ones. Through the power of the Holy Spirit and the Word of God, God will break and destroy the yoke of sin and bondage (Nahum 1:13).

The reality is Jesus has made every born again believer free and who the Son makes free remains free as long as we rely totally on Him (John 8:36). The Apostle Paul reminds believers that we are adopted by God and did not receive the spirit of bondage unto fear (Romans 8:15). He also admonishes believers not to submit or be a slave again to bondage standing in our Christ given freedom (Galatians 5:1). Believers remain free by embracing the truth of the Word of the Lord and taking authority over bondage and declaring freedom.

Because bondage is a spirit, it can only be destroyed by spiritual weaponry. Believers must make a declaration of war against the spirit of bondage with the spoken Word. The sent Word of God will rescue from the pit of destruction and contend with darkness producing deliverance in the believer's life and their loved ones. With this intention, begin to declare the spoken Word.

For unsaved children, declare I am righteous and my seed shall be delivered.

… the seed of the righteous shall be delivered (Proverbs 11:21b).

But thus saith the Lord, Even the captives of the mighty shall be taken away, and the prey of the terrible shall be delivered: for I will contend with him that contendeth with thee, and I will save thy children (Isaiah 49:25).

For an unsaved household, declare because I believe in Jesus and my house shall be saved.

And they answered, Believe in the Lord Jesus Christ (give yourself up to Him, take yourself out of your own keeping and entrust yourself into His keeping), and you will be saved, and this applies both to you and your household as well (Acts 16:31, AMP Version).

For believers dealing with habits or struggles, declare I will embrace my freedom in Jesus.

And you will know the Truth, and the Truth will set you free (John 8:32, AMP Version).

So if the Son liberates you (makes you free men), then you are really and unquestionably free (John 8:36, AMP Version).

I am the Lord your God, Who has brought you out of Egypt, out of the house of bondage (Exodus 20:2, AMP Version).

God is my strong Fortress; He guides the blameless in His way and sets him free (2 Samuel 22:33, AMP Version)

But as many as received him, to them gave he power to become the sons of God (John 1:12a).

The aforementioned were just a few Scriptures to start the process of proclaiming the spoken Word in your situation.

As I stated earlier, employing the weapon of the Sword of the Word is a coupling of spoken and written. The written Word is important and we must accept the Word of God as the truth. When we receive the Word of God as the truth, it works effectively in us (1 Thessalonians 2:13). Therefore, it is critical to do as Joshua encourages us to do and meditate on the Word day and night to be successful (Joshua 1:8).

As believers, not only must we know the Word of God; but, we must know the Word in correct context. By knowing the Word of God in correct context, it will ensure an effective impact against Satan and his cohorts. Do not forget, Satan knows the Word; however, he will misrepresent the meaning and context every time. He does this to produce confusion and make us question or doubt the Word of God. Knowing the correct context of the Word of God opens our understanding. When believers understand the written Word of God, we want to obey the Word. Furthermore, our spirit is built in faith and we know how to apply the Word to our lives. This is significant because Satan is always testing the Word of God and tempting believers to walk in disobedience. An example of Satan in action is revealed in the book of Genesis.

In Genesis chapter two, with the exception of one tree, God informed Adam that he could freely eat of every tree in the Garden of Eden. The one tree God gave Adam direct command not to eat was the tree of the knowledge of good and evil. The reasons why Adam could not eat of that specific tree was because he would spiritually die, would no longer live a life of innocence, and would be aware of the knowledge of sin (2:16-17). Directly after, God gave Adam a wife named Eve.

In Chapter 3:1-6, Satan approaches Eve to test the Word of God given to Adam. First, Satan suggests to Eve that God did not mean what He said. Second, Satan convinced Eve that she would not die. Thirdly, Satan appealed to what John refers to as the lust of the flesh, lust of eyes, and the pride of life (1 John 2:16). Genesis 3:5-6 (AMP Version) provides details of the conversation between Satan, Adam, and Eve.

For God knows that in the day you eat of it your eyes will be opened and you will be like God, knowing the difference between good and evil and blessing and calamity (5). This is the pride of life.

And when the woman saw that the tree was good (suitable and pleasant) for food and that it was delightful to look at, and a tree to be desired in order to make one wise, she took of its fruit and ate; and she gave some also to her husband, and he ate (6). This is the lust of eyes and flesh.

Adam and Eve failed the test of obedience to the Word of God because they listened to a liar and murderer instead of believing the truth (John 8:44).

Jesus and the Weapon of the Word of God

What do the actions of Adam and Eve have to do with the weapon of the written Word? Due to their disobedience, mankind was separated from God and Satan became the god of this world. As the god of this world, his strategy has not changed from the days of Adam and Eve. He attempted to test Jesus in every point that he tried Adam. In fact, God allowed Satan to test Jesus in the same areas as Adam to redeem and reconcile every believer unto Himself (Romans 5:10). Where Adam failed in disobedience, Jesus passed in obedience by applying the weapon of the written Word (Romans 5:19). What is so awesome about the aforementioned statement is Jesus taught believers by example how to operate and incorporate the weapon of the Word in spiritual warfare. Matthew chapter 4:1-11 (AMP Version) renders a step by step account of how Jesus skillfully applied the Sword of the written Word.

Then Jesus was led (guided) by the Holy Spirit into the wilderness (desert) to be tempted (tested and tried) by the devil. And He went without food for forty days and forty nights, and later He was hungry (1, 2).

And the tempter came and said to Him. If You are God's Son, command these stones to be made loaves of bread. But He replied, It has been written, Man shall not live and be upheld and sustained by bread alone, but by every word that comes forth from the mouth of God (3, 4).

After going without food for forty days and nights, Jesus was hungry. In obedience to God, He followed the leading of the Holy Spirit into the wilderness or desert to be tested. Jesus, the Word, was on a divine assignment in the wilderness as the Son of man. Believers, the wilderness/desert is the place where only you and God will dwell. The desert is where spiritual warfare in raw form takes place. There is a mental battle and every Word God has spoken over your life or written prophetically about your destiny is being tried. The devil will declare the wilderness is where God left us to die, but God will say the wilderness is where He prepared us for destiny and taught us how to live.

Having said that, in the first test Satan's ploy was designed to cause Jesus to step into divinity from Jesus the Son of man by requesting He supernaturally turn stones into bread. Satan assumed that Jesus was weak in his flesh and so desperate for food that He would reveal his divinity out of season. By posing the statement, "if You are the Son of God," Satan validates the fact that he knew Jesus as the Son of God. Because of hunger Jesus was weak in His flesh, but His Spirit was strong. He reminded Satan of the written Word declared in Deuteronomy 8:3. Jesus made it clear to Satan His priority is to fulfill His divine assignment. Despite, his fleshly desire for food, consuming natural food is not the only thing that sustains a Spirit-filled believer. Jesus insists that the Word of God has greater sustaining power for life. Why? He, the Word, is the Bread of Life and Living Water (John 6:35).

In the second test, Satan did something that he always attempts to do in spiritual warfare. What does he attempt to do? He misuses the Word of God by quoting Scriptures out of context.

> *Then the devil took Him into the holy city and placed Him on a turret (pinnacle, gable) of the temple sanctuary. And he said to Him, If You are the Son of God, throw Yourself down; for it is written, He will give His angels charge over you, and they will bear you up on their hands, lest you strike your foot against a stone. Jesus said to him, On the other hand, it is written also, you shall not tempt, test thoroughly, or try exceedingly the Lord your God (Matthew 4: 5-7, AMP Version).*

In the text above, Satan misquoted Psalm 91:11-12 to convince Jesus to commit suicide. If Jesus as Son of man threw Himself to His death, His divine purpose to redeem man and destroy the kingdom of darkness would not have been fulfilled.

Believers, we must be careful in spiritual warfare to recognize when Satan distorts the Word of God to encourage behaviors unbecoming as believers to walk in deliberate disobedience. Satan will appear to carry you to the pinnacle just to separate you from purpose, destiny, and God's grace. If Satan succeeds, the believer will commit spiritual suicide while tempting the God of our eternity. Remember, Jesus in His humanity had the same tools He has given to the believer to defeat Satan. He was full of the Holy Spirit and full of the Word. As He did in the first test, Jesus drew the Sword of the written Word as His weapon stating, "It is written you shall not test God (Deuteronomy 6:16)."

In the final test, Satan promised Jesus the world if He would just worship him:

Again, the devil took Him up on a very high mountain and showed Him all the kingdoms of the world and the glory (the splendor, magnificence, preeminence, and excellence) of them. And he said to Him, These things, all taken together, I will give You, if You will prostrate Yourself before me and do homage and worship me. Then Jesus said to him, Begone, Satan! For it has been written, You shall worship the Lord your God and

Him alone shall you serve. Then the devil departed from Him, and behold, angels came and ministered to Him (Matthew 4:8-11, AMP Version).

How ridiculous and appalling for Satan to think because Jesus appeared weak as Son of man that He would bow to him. Jesus is still God the Son and **Satan's creator** (John 1:3). In addition, what Satan was offering to Jesus was already His. What is awesome about this discourse is Jesus made a decision that this test is over! He dismissed Satan with authority quoting once again the Word (Deuteronomy 6:13). Jesus reminded Satan that He will only worship His Father rendering service unto Him alone. Jesus was tested in every area of humanity, but He did not sin (Hebrews 2:18, 4:15).

In all three instances, Jesus employed the Word of God correctly and skillfully to combat the mental spiritual warfare of Satan. Satan's whole purpose in the wilderness was to have a repeat of the Garden of Eden. However, even in the wilderness, God knew that the weapon of His Word would not fail. Satan had no choice but to leave Jesus alone. Immediately, God sent ministering angels to strengthen Jesus.

Believers of God, Jesus has given us His Word as a principal weapon to remain in total victory. Decide today that you will follow the example of Jesus utilizing the indispensable sword of the Spirit.

In spiritual warfare, speak what is written penetrating every dimension of darkness ruining Satan's attempts to attack your mind, spirit, family, finances, ministry, and destiny. In the same manner as Jesus, God will send ministering angels to strengthen you in the midst of and after the test.

Weapons for Spiritual Warfare The Weapon of the Word

Chapter Two Review

1. Why is the Word of God fundamental?

_____

_____

_____

2. How is the Word of God described?

_____

_____

_____

3. Where should the Word be hidden?

_____

4. Why is it important to be skillful in the knowledge and application of the Word?

_____

5. Is the Bible an ordinary literary book?

_____

6. What does 2 Timothy 3:16 and 2 Peter 1:20-21 states?

_____

_____

7. Why is it important to know how the Word of God originated?

8. What does the Word of God teach believers?

9. How should believers approach the Word?

10. Who is the best person to ask for understanding of the Word of God?

11. What should you do when Satan tells you that you cannot read the Word?

12. What can the Sword of the Word do?

13. What does the Sword of the Word do in spiritual warfare?

14. When the Word is spoken, what happens?

15. Where does the Holy Spirit put power for believers to speak God's Word?

16. Is the Word alive?

17. Who makes the Word manifest in a situation?

18. For those who believe, does Jesus heal sickness and disease?

Weapons for Spiritual Warfare | The Weapon of the Word

19. Who did Luke reveal was healed by Jesus' Word?

_____

_____

20. What did the centurion ask Jesus to do to heal his servant?

_____

21. What did Luke 13:11-13 (AMP Version) call sickness?

_____

_____

22. How was the woman noticed by Jesus?

_____

_____

23. Where does worship take place?

_____

24. What areas do the spirits of lack and bondage affect believers' lives?

_____

_____

25. How do believers remain free?

_____

_____

26. What does Satan do with the Word?

_____

27. Why did Adam and Eve fall?

_____

28. How did Jesus defeat Satan in the wilderness?

_____

_____

29. Where is the battle taking place between Jesus and Satan?

_____

30. Why does the Word have greater sustaining power for life?

_____

_____

31. What was Satan attempting to do in the second test with Jesus?

_____

_____

32. Do believers have to endure test in their lives forever or is there a season of rest?

_____

_____

Chapter Three

The Weapon of the Name of Jesus

Wherefore God also hath highly exalted him, and given him a name which is above every name: That at the name of Jesus every knee should bow, of things in heaven, and things in earth, and things under the earth (Philippians 2:9-10).

From Holy Ghost conception, He was introduced as the Son of God and given the name Jesus (Luke 1:31-32). Jesus in Hebrew is the word Yeshua. Yeshua means "Yahweh saves or is salvation."[8] The name prophetically proclaims His purpose and assignment to save His people and the world from the power of sin while empowering those who believe to walk in power as sons of God (Matthew 1:21, John 1:12). God the Father made a declaration that the name of Jesus is exalted above every name and everyone must bow to the name of Jesus whether in heaven, earth, or hell (Philippians 2:10). As believers, knowing how to implement the name of Jesus in spiritual warfare against the kingdom of darkness is pertinent to our spiritual life. It is only in the name of Jesus that there is

---

[8.] Donald C. Stamps and John W. Adams., eds. *King James Version Life in the Spirit Study Bible* (1992; repr, Grand Rapids: Zondervan, 2005), 1405.

life, salvation, faith, justification, and power. Also, because they believe, demons tremble at the name of Jesus (James 2:19).

There is life in Jesus' Name for those who Believe

There is life only through Jesus. Jesus declares, "I am the Bread of Life that gives life–the Living Bread (John 6:48, AMP Version)." What does life in Jesus entail? As stated in chapter three, Adam's disobedience had a great impact on mankind. It is also how the devil gained control and sin entered into human nature. Because sin is of the devil, the Son of God was manifested to "undo, destroy, loosen, and dissolve" the works the devil has done through sin (1 John 3:8b, AMP Version). Adam's actions revealed there is a penalty or wage for sin. That penalty is death. This death was natural, spiritual, and eternal. Believing in the name of Jesus as the gift of God and receiving Him produces life eternally (Romans 6:23). The Apostle John explains that this life in the name of Jesus is given to everyone who believes:

> *For God so loved the world that He gave His only begotten Son, that whosoever believeth in Him should not perish, but have everlasting life (John 3:16).*

But these are written (recorded) in order that you may believe that Jesus is the Christ (the Anointed One), the Son of God, and through believing and cleaving to and trusting and relying upon Him you may have life through (in) His name through who He is (John 20:31, AMP Version).

And this is that testimony (that evidence): God gave us eternal life, and this life is in His Son. He who possesses the Son has that life; he who does not possess the Son of God does not have that life. I write this to you who believe in (adhere to, trust in, and rely on) the name of the Son of God (in the peculiar services and blessings conferred by Him on men), so that you may know with settled and absolute knowledge that you already have life, yes, eternal life (1 John 5:11-13, AMP Version).

In the text, the Apostle John differentiates those who believe and possess Jesus from those who do not believe and possess Jesus. Those who believe possessing Jesus are guaranteed life in His name. Those who do not believe in Jesus and do not possess Him are without life. In spiritual warfare, embracing the truth regarding eternal life in the name of Jesus is essential for believers. The reason why is because believers who embrace that we have eternal life in Jesus receive hope in this natural life to live without the fear of death or functioning in sin as a lifestyle. Moreover, by understanding this revelation, we boldly do all things in word or deed in the name of Jesus (Colossians 3:17a, AMP Version). This includes proclaiming the name of Jesus to destroy demonic activity on every hand.

There is Faith and Salvation in the Name of Jesus

Again, doing everything in the name of Jesus begins with having faith or belief. God has commanded that believers should believe on the name of Jesus (1 John 3:23). The reason why is because Jesus is the Author and the Finisher of our faith (Hebrews 12:2). Faith in Jesus' name makes those who believe whole and changes their lives. The Apostle Peter speaking about the miracle at the gate of the temple called Beautiful states that it was through the name of Jesus that the man was healed.

> *And His name, through and by faith in His name, has this man whom you see and recognize well and strong. Yes, the faith which is through and by Him (Jesus) has given the man this perfect soundness of body before all of you (Acts 3:16, AMP Version).*

The name of Jesus is the Way to Salvation

In the Word of God, salvation refers to safety, deliverance, rescue, and dominion from the power of sin through Jesus Christ.[9] In addition, this salvation is offered freely to everyone who repents embracing faith in God through Jesus alone.

> *This Jesus is the Stone which was despised and rejected by you, the builders, but which has become the Head of the corner (the Cornerstone). And there is salvation in and through no one else; for there is no other name under heaven given among men by and in which we must be saved (Acts 4:11-12, AMP Version).*

> *That if thou shalt confess with thy mouth the Lord Jesus, and shalt believe in thine heart that God hath raised Him from the dead, thou shalt be saved. For with the heart man believeth unto righteousness, and with the mouth confession is made unto salvation (Romans 10:9-10).*

This is important in the warfare against false teaching or doctrine. Satan has convinced many that they can have a relationship with God without

---

[9] Merrill F. Unger. *Unger's Bible Dictionary* (Chicago: Moody Press, 1977), 1114, s.v., "salvation."

Jesus. However, Jesus makes us aware that there is no relationship with God without Him. In the book of John Jesus said, "I am the Way, the Truth, and the Life, no one comes to the Father except by (through) Me (John 14:6, AMP Version)." Therefore, when someone states that he or she can know God the Father without Jesus; believers have to give them the truth in love.

Salvation in Jesus' name generates life, not death and hope, not condemnation. Just as Jesus did not come to condemn, believers do not condemn the person. While displaying the love of Jesus to the person, believers have to take authority over the demonic spirit assigned to destroy that person's life in Jesus' name. John 3:17-18 states the heart of God regarding salvation in Jesus' name:

> *For God sent not His Son into the world to condemn the world; but that the world through Him might be saved. He that believeth on Him is not condemned: but he that believeth not is condemned already, because he hath not believeth in the name of the only begotten Son of God.*

Take note that Jesus nor believers condemn anyone; however, the person rejecting salvation in the name of Jesus has sentenced condemnation upon him or herself.

When we believe there is salvation in the name of Jesus, He rescues everyone who believes from unrighteous behaviors and attitudes and justifies or declares we are in right standing with God. Although the penalty of sin is deserved, Jesus declares believers are not guilty and makes us the righteousness of God through Him (2 Corinthians 5:21). Why is justification in Jesus' name so important? It is important because having right standing with God means believers are reconciled to Him through Jesus.

And all things are of God, who hath reconciled us to himself by Jesus Christ, and hath given to us the ministry of reconciliation; To wit, that God was in Christ reconciling the world unto himself, not imputing their trespasses unto them; and hath committed unto us the word of reconciliation (2 Corinthians 5:18-19) .

Remember, anyone committing sin is of the devil and believers cannot give him space (1 John 3:8a, Ephesians 4:27). Satan attempts to deceive believers that the way we live our lives does not matter. It matters for two reasons: separation and operation. First, sin separates believers from God and inheriting the kingdom of God. After naming several things in 1 Corinthians 6:9-10 that will prevent any unrighteous person from inheriting the kingdom of God, Paul explains in 1 Corinthians 6:11 that believers are justified in the name of Jesus.

And such were some of you: but ye are washed, but ye are sanctified, but ye are justified in the name of the Lord Jesus, and by the Spirit of our God.

According to the Apostle Paul, believing in the name of Jesus provokes change in the lives of those who believe. Believers do not continue to live in unrighteousness because we will lose our Godly inheritance. We are washed by the Word of God and sanctified or set apart unto God obtaining right standing with God in the name of Jesus.

The second reason why it is important for a believer to live a sin free lifestyle is the operation of the name of Jesus in spiritual warfare. Satan is not intimidated by anyone whose life he has a strong foothold or dwelling place within. As believers, we are given authority over Satan and his cohorts. Living a sin free lifestyle and not practicing sin, keeps believers connected to Jesus freeing us to operate in the power of His name walking in great authority against the power of darkness.

Power in the Name of Jesus

Jesus informs every believer that in order to receive anything from God the Father, we must pray in His name. Because He is our Mediator, Advocator, and High Priest, He sits at the right hand of the Father interceding on our behalf in everything (Romans 8:34, Hebrews 4:14, 1 John 2:1). All authority or power has been given to Jesus in heaven and earth (Matthew 28:18). In addition, He has given every believer authority to pray and operate in the power of His name.

I assure you, most solemnly I tell you, if anyone steadfastly believes in Me, he will himself be able to do the things that I do; and he will do even greater things than these, because I go to the Father. And I will do (I Myself will grant) whatever you ask in My name (as presenting all that I AM), so that the Father may be glorified and extolled in (through) the Son. Yes, I will grant (I Myself will do for you) whatever you shall ask in My name as presenting all that I AM (John 14:12-14, AMP Version).

As I stated in chapter two when discussing prayer, prayer is how we access power with God in Jesus' name. Jesus takes it a step further. By praying in His name, Jesus informs believers that we can operate in His power doing greater works than He did because we are filled with His Spirit. Furthermore, those who believe in His name will function supernaturally in signs and wonders dismantling demonic activity and He will grant whatever we ask in His name.

And these signs shall follow them that believe, In my name shall they cast out devils, they shall speak with new tongues; They shall take up serpents, and if they drink any deadly thing, it shall not hurt them, they shall lay hands on the sick and they shall recover (Mark 16:17-18).

When believers operate in the full authority Jesus released in His name, devils tremble, fear departs, and the Holy Spirit flows healing the sick and raising the dead. If Satan dispatches his demons to hurt or harm believers in any way, his plots are canceled. Believers who employ the weapon of Jesus' name must believe and be strong. This is not for those who are fearful and immature in the Spirit, but mature believers who allow Jesus to operate through them in spiritual warfare.

Devils recognize the power in the name of Jesus and respond to the command of being cast out (Matthew 8:29-32). Satan knows who operates in the power of Jesus' name and who does not. In the book of Acts chapters sixteen and nineteen, there are accounts of this fact. The first account takes place Acts chapter 16:16-18 (AMP Version) describes the events of Paul casting out the spirit of divination:

> *As we were on our way to the place of prayer, we were met by a slave girl who was possessed by a spirit of divination claiming to foretell future events and to discover hidden knowledge and she brought her owners much gain by her fortunetelling (16).*

She kept following Paul and the rest of us, shouting loudly, These men are the servants of the Most High God! They announce to you the way of salvation! (17).

And she did this for many days. Then Paul, being sorely annoyed and worn out, turned and said to the spirit within her, I charge you in the name of Jesus Christ to come out of her! And it came out that very moment (18).

On the surface, the young lady appears innocent. The problem is her occupation was a witch. She operated under the spirit of witchcraft and divination as a fortuneteller. Attempting to appear connected to the Apostles, she followed them announcing that "these are servants of the Most High God!" Although what she was speaking was true because demons recognize those who name the name of Jesus, she was not of God.

Satan always attempts to mimic the Holy Spirit's attributes. Believers are to try the spirit by the Spirit because the Spirit of God bears witness with Himself (1 John 4:1, 1 John 5:6-8). The Apostle Paul's spirit did not bear witness with her as truth. In fact, verse eighteen states, "he was annoyed." The demon operating in the girl vexed Paul's spirit. Therefore, utilizing the name of Jesus, Paul cast the devil out of her.

How do we know that the demon knew Paul's authority to operate in the name of Jesus? The spirit of divination came out that very moment. Paul believed in the name of Jesus and received the expected outcome. Simultaneously, he set the girl free from the bondage of divination and the men controlling her for money.

In Acts chapter 19:13-17 (Amp Version), the events of the second accounts unfolds when the sons of Sceva attempted to cast out an evil spirit.

Then some of the traveling Jewish exorcists (men who adjure evil spirits) also undertook to call the name of the Lord Jesus over those who had evil spirits, saying, I solemnly implore and charge you by the Jesus Whom Paul preaches!(13).

Seven sons of a certain Jewish chief priest named Sceva were doing this. But one evil spirit retorted, Jesus I know, and Paul I know about, but who are you? (14-15).

Then the man in whom the evil dwelt leaped upon them, mastering two of them, and was so violent against them that they dashed out of that house in fear, stripped naked and wounded (16).

This became known to all who lived in Ephesus, both Jews and Greeks, and alarm and terror fell upon them all; and the name of the Lord Jesus was extolled and magnified (17).

From these passages of Scriptures, two things are evident. First, unless you are a spirit-filled believer of Jesus Christ, you cannot operate in the authority of His name. The reason why is because Jesus renders revelation and understanding to the significance of His name to those who believe and through His Holy Spirit renders the power to operate (Mark 16:17, Acts 1:8).

Secondly, the evil spirit spoke to the sons of Sceva stating, "Jesus I know, and Paul I know, but who are you?" This statement confirms that Satan recognizes those who are sealed by the Holy Spirit and belong to Jesus. The spirit knew Jesus and Paul by name. The same is true for believers that tap in spiritual dimensions of the power in Jesus' name dismantling the influences of darkness. The devils know your name. The good news is Luke 10:17 declares devils are subject to the Jesus in you because there is power in His name!

Power at the Mention of the Name of Jesus

The very mention of the name of Jesus is packed with so much power that it shifts atmospheres. In anointed worship services, Jesus' name saturates the atmosphere with God's presence. Through the Holy Spirit deliverance occurs instantly to all who will open their hearts to receive His presence.

In view of the fact that there is active power in the name of Jesus, there is continuous warfare from the kingdom of darkness to influence the earthly realm not to mention His name. Jesus commanded that believers preach the Gospel to the entire world (Mark 16:15). The Apostles obeyed Jesus. Because everything they did was in the name of Jesus, they had to endure much persecution. The earthly officials ordered the Apostles not to preach, teach, heal, or mention the name of Jesus. Despite being imprisoned and beaten, the Apostles continued to exalt the name of Jesus.

Acts 4:14-18, 5:40 (AMP Version) reveals exactly how these actions occurred.

> *And since they saw the man who had been cured standing there beside them, they could not contradict the fact or say anything in opposition. But having ordered the prisoners to go aside out of the council chamber, they conferred (debated) among themselves (14-15).*

> *Saying, what are we to do with these men? For that an extraordinary miracle has been performed by (through) them is plain to all the residents of Jerusalem, and we cannot deny it (16).*

> *But in order that it may not spread further among the people and the nation, let us warn and forbid them with a stern threat not to speak any more to anyone in this name or about this Person (17).*

> *So they summoned them and imperatively instructed them not to converse in any way or teach at all in or about the name of Jesus (18).*

> *.... and summoning the apostles, they flogged them and sternly forbade them to speak in or about the name of Jesus, and allowed them to go (5:40).*

The Apostles did not bow down to the threats charging them not to mention the name of Jesus. The officials reasoning was a direct demonic assault manifesting in the natural to hinder the Gospel from spreading among the people and nation.

Today, Christians are living in a culture quite similar to the times of the Apostles. To take a stand against the spirit of compromise defending the name of Jesus comes with great persecution. Under the umbrella of being politically correct, not operating in the spirit of offense, or excluding people, Satan attempts to influence and convince some believers to compromise mentioning the name of Jesus in worship service or prayer. The ministry of music psalmist replaces Jesus' name in a song with a sensual sound that will crossover secularly.

In the worldly societal functions where Christians are requested to pray publicly, it is alright for Christians to mention the name of our Father, God, in the name of God, Your name, Jehovah, and Yahweh without repercussion. In addition, religious people who worship other gods can say the names of their god with no repercussion. However, the name of Jesus provokes a backlash of offense from the powers of darkness influencing the earthly realm.

Believers, remember Satan and the powers of darkness respond to those who operate boldly in the name of Jesus. We cannot afford to surrender such a mighty weapon to be politically correct. If believers surrender to political correctness, weakness will reign and Satan will attempt to wreak havoc in the earthly realm against the kingdom of God. Jesus gives us strength to stand in the midst of compromise and persecution. Jesus is greater in us than what is taking place in the world (1 John 4:4). Thank God for non-compromising believers who understand Jesus is a mighty power working in us by His Spirit.

And so that you can know and understand what is the immeasurable and unlimited and surpassing greatness of His power in and for us who believe, as demonstrated in the working of His mighty strength (Ephesians 1:19, AMP Version).

No Greater Name than the Name of Jesus

The reality is God the Father does not require anyone to exalt His name, but His Son's. God the Father always points us to Jesus and Jesus always points us to the Father. Therefore, by exalting Jesus, God is exalted and receives the glory. God the Father gave this honor to His Son. The superiority of the name of Jesus is greater than angels (Hebrews 1:4). God the Father sat Jesus at His right hand in heavenly places (Ephesians 1:20). God the Father declared His authority higher than any other name and made everything subject to his authority.

Far above all rule and authority and power and dominion and every name that is named above every title that can be conferred not only in this age and in this world, but also in the age and the world which are to come. And He has put all things under His feet and has appointed Him the universal and supreme Head of the church (Ephesians 1:21-22, AMP Version).

Believers of God, every situation, circumstance, or demonic force that would rise against us is subject to the name of Jesus! Be relentless to utilize Jesus' name knowing there is no name greater given to the believer. Some examples of how to utilize the name of Jesus in spiritual warfare are found on pages 34-35, 135-137, 233-234.

Chapter Three Review

1. What does Romans 6:23 say?

2. What happens when believers embrace eternal life in Jesus?

3. What does Acts 4:12 say?

4. What is the false teaching of Satan regarding having a relationship with God?

5. Does Jesus condemn a person?

6. Who does a person belong to when he or she commit sin?

7. Why is it important for believers to live right not practicing a lifestyle of sin?

8. Is Satan intimidated by believers practicing a lifestyle of sin?

9. When applying the weapon of the name of Jesus, what is the connection to prayer?

10. What does Mark 16:17-18 say?

11. What happens when a believer operates in the full authority of the name of Jesus?

12. Do devils recognize the name of Jesus?

13. What type of spirit was the girl in the Acts 16 text operating in?

14. What did the demon do to Paul's spirit?

15. How do we know that the demon knew Paul's authority?

16. What were the sons of Sceva attempting perform in Jesus' name?

17. What were the two lessons learned from what the sons of Sceva did?

18. Do devils know your name?

19. What does Jesus' name accomplish in an atmosphere?

20. What is the continuous warfare about from the kingdom of darkness regarding the name of Jesus?

21. What happened to the Apostles for using the name of Jesus?

22. What happens today when Christians use the name of Jesus?

___

___

23. If we surrender the name of Jesus, what will take place in the earthly realm?

___

___

___

24. Is there any name greater than Jesus?

___

Chapter Four

The Weapon of the Blood

Neither by the blood of goats and calves, but by his own blood he entered in once into the holy place, having obtained eternal redemption for us (Hebrews 9:12). But you were purchased with the precious blood of Christ the Messiah, like that of a sacrificial lamb without blemish or spot (1Peter 1:19, AMP Version). And they overcame him by the blood of the Lamb (Revelation 12:11).

Even as the blood flowing through the veins of our bodies is vital, the blood of Jesus is vital in the flow of our spiritual life and is a lethal weapon in spiritual warfare. Whereas the Old Testament covenant or Law was sealed by the blood of animals that atoned sin, Jesus offering Himself as a sacrifice sealed the New Testament covenant with His blood removing sin. The blood of Jesus has a great impact in spiritual warfare because it encompasses remission and cleansing of sins, redemption, reconciliation, and peace with God. Furthermore, believers are purchased, sealed, and covered by the blood to live victoriously.

According to God, life and atonement was in the blood (Leviticus 17:11). Jesus informed us that there is no life except we drink His blood (John 6:53). The Old Testament or Law was given to Israel by cleansing everything by the blood, water, and hyssop including the book of the Law, the tabernacle, the vessels, and the people (Hebrews 9:19-20). Neither the priests nor the people could have a covenant relationship with God or enter God's presence with sin. Therefore, the shedding of the blood and sacrifice of goats, calves, lambs, and turtle doves was significant as an atoning offering for the remitting sins of the priests and the people (Hebrews 9:22).

The ordinance of atonement took place once a year and was only a temporary resolution for sin. In addition, the blood sacrifice of the animals only covered the sins of the people. However, God had a greater purpose. He desired a better covenant relationship with His people and their sins forgiven because sin provoked the wrath of God. Therefore, God's desire was not to cover sin; however, He desired to remove the nature of sin from the lives of His people. Neither the imperfect blood sacrifices of animals nor the imperfect priests presenting the sacrifice could fulfill His desire. The reason why is the blood of animal sacrifices did not have the power to accomplish the task of taking away sins or the sinful nature.

For the law having a shadow of good things to come, and not the very image of the things, can never with those sacrifices which they offered year by year continually make the comers thereunto perfect. For then would they not have ceased to be offered? because that the worshippers once purged should have had no more conscience of sins. But in those sacrifices there is a remembrance again made of sins every year. For it is not possible that the blood of bulls and of goats should take away sins (Hebrews 10:1-4).

Therefore, in order to fulfill His desire, God needed a blood sacrifice that was better than that of goats, turtle doves, and calves. God searched for a sinless sacrifice to stand in the gap for humanity. With this perfect sinless sacrifice, the blood offering would remove the nature, penalty, influence, and power of sin forever. The only person with the qualifications to fulfill the purpose of God for humanity was His only Son, Jesus (Hebrews 9:26).

Jesus who was sinless took the sins of the world upon Himself experiencing life in human form (Hebrews 2:17, 4:15). According to Romans 8:3, God sent Jesus in the likeness of sinful flesh for sin to condemn or attack the nature of sin. Fulfilling the Law, Jesus became High Priest and the sacrificial Lamb without spot or blemish. John 1:29b declares, "Behold the Lamb of God, which taketh away the sin of the world." Hebrews 7:27, 9:14a, 10:5-14 reveals how Jesus offered Himself as our blood sacrifice.

> *Who needeth not daily, as those high priests, to offer up sacrifice, first for his own sins, and then for the people's: for this he did once, when he offered up himself (Hebrews 7:27).*

> *How much more shall the blood of Christ who through the eternal Spirit offered himself without spot to God (Hebrews 9:14a).*

> *Wherefore when he cometh into the world, he saith, Sacrifice and offering thou wouldest not, but a body hast thou prepared me: In burnt offerings and sacrifices for sin thou hast had no pleasure. Then said I, Lo I come in the volume of the book it is written of me, to do thy will, O God (Hebrews 10:5-7).*

> *By the which will we are sanctified through the offering of the body of Jesus Christ once for all. And every priest standeth daily ministering and*

offering oftentimes the same sacrifices, which can never take away sins: But this man, after he had offered one sacrifice for sins forever, sat down on the right hand of God. From henceforth expecting till his enemies be made his footstool. For by one offering he hath perfected forever them that are sanctified (Hebrews 10:10-14).

By becoming the testator that gave His life, Jesus fulfilled the will of God. A testator is a person who dies leaving a will or testament.[10] As the testator, Jesus' death yields power. His blood is effective rendering through Him a New Testament covenant that is enforceable for the kingdom of God (Hebrews 9:16-17). In this new blood covenant, anyone who accepts Jesus as his/her personal Savior has the Law of God written in his/her heart and mind receiving an eternal inheritance (Hebrews 10:16).

Why is the history of the blood sacrifice so important to spiritual warfare? The history is important because the blood of Jesus has a solid foundation. The Holy Spirit bears witness to the validity of the power

---

[10] *Merriam-Webster.com*, n.d., s.v., "testator," accessed February 15, 2018. https://www.merriam-webster.com/dictionary/testator.

of the blood that made Jesus the only Mediator between man and God (1 John 5:6, Hebrews 9:15). Jesus' blood has triumphant power over sin and Satan making it the believers' most potent weapon.

When believers have faith in the power of the blood of Jesus accepting Him as our High Priest, we boldly enter into the presence of God embracing everything the applied blood of Jesus entails in our lives (Hebrews 10:19). There is not one area in the lives of believers that the blood of Jesus does not touch. Due to the fact that the blood of Jesus is multi-purposeful spiritually in lives of believers, Satan and his cohorts cannot penetrate pass the blood without permission from God or the uncovered believer. Every time Satan sees a true believer, He sees the blood of Jesus saturating his or her life.

As believers, we really do not realize we are untouchable in the blood of Jesus. The untouchable component is powerful in spiritual warfare because the impact of the accomplishments of the blood of Jesus yields victory in our lives. As previously stated in the first paragraph, the blood encompasses remission, redemption, and cleansing of sins;

reconciliation and peace with God; and believers are purchased, sealed, and covered by the blood.

Remission, Cleansing, and Redemption of sins

One major impact of the blood covenant for believers is the remission of sins. According to the *International Standard Bible Encyclopedia Online (ISBE)*, remission is exemption from the consequences of an offense and forgiveness.[11] When Satan or anyone attempts to remind God of a believer's past life or sins that have been forgiven, God does not even hold a conversation because He does not remember them. The blood of Jesus has sin eraseability power.

> *And their sins and iniquities will I remember no more. Now where remission of these is, there is no more offering for sin (Hebrews 10:17-18).*

Remember, in the Old Testament sins were remembered every year at atonement. However, the New Testament sealed by the blood of Jesus produces total forgiveness of sins and iniquities or inherent sins. In turn,

---

[11.] James Orr, ed. *International Standard Bible Encyclopedia*, s.v. "remission," accessed July 20, 2012, http://www.internationalstandardbible.com.

God declares them forgotten forever. By His blood producing forgiveness, Jesus our propitiator conciliated God's wrath placing everyone who believes in right standing with God (Romans 3:25). Praises be to God that Jesus' blood is sufficient as the final offering on the behalf of our sins. This truth is so essential because Satan cannot hold any believer in bondage to sin.

Not only does the blood of Jesus remit or forgive sins, it also cleanses the residue of sin. What exactly does it mean to be cleansed by the blood? It means Jesus' blood washes and purifies removing sin from the lives of everyone who believes and remains in the light of God.

But if we really are living and walking in the Light as he (Himself) is in the Light, we have (true, unbroken) fellowship on with one another and the blood of Jesus Christ His Son cleanses (removes) us from all sin and guilt, (keeps us cleansed from sin in all its forms and manifestations) (I John 1:7, AMP Version).

And from Jesus Christ, who is the faithful witness, and the first begotten of the dead, and the prince of the kings of the earth. Unto him that loved us and washed us from our sins in his own blood (Revelation 1:5).

Satan does not want any believer to truly understand that the blood of Jesus performed a complete work destroying the power of sin. The blood has the power to break, cleanse, and destroy every yoke, every habit, every spirit of infirmity, every spirit of addiction (nicotine, alcohol, drugs, and overeating), and every spirit of uncleanness and perversion in every form that it may present itself (profanity, pornography, fornication, adultery, homosexuality, lesbianism, masturbation, anxiety, and false teaching). Knowing and embracing the blood's cleansing power liberates believers from every spirit of the bondage of sin, the guilt, the desire to serve sin, and the residue of sin.

Without the residue, Satan does not have access nor can trace his past influence that once held everyone captive because the blood of Jesus redeems. Ephesians 1:7a (AMP Version) states, "In Him we have redemption, deliverance, and salvation through His blood..." To redeem or redemption means to tear loose or rescue (ISBE online).[12] Notice in the definition, redemption is two-fold. First, redemption in the blood tears, literally rips, every believer out of any demonic attack loosing every stronghold that Satan attempts to plant. Second, redemption in the blood rescues or saves believers from past, present, and future situations continually as long as we remain locked into Jesus.

Believers never have to worry about the darts, schemes, and plots the devil and his cohorts attempt to throw at or set against us, anyone, or anything connected to us. The same Jesus that rescued us from eternal death has prophesied that He will rescue every one that hopes in the work of His blood from every threat of the kingdom of darkness.

> *For it is He Who rescued and saved us from such a perilous death, and He will still rescue and save us; in and on Him we have set our hope (our joyful and confident expectation) that He will again deliver us from danger and destruction and draw us to Himself (2 Corinthians 1:10, AMP Version).*

[12.] ibid, s.v. "redemption"

If the redemption of believers came by the way of silver, gold, or vain tradition, there would be no hope or confidence in the blood; however, the great news is our redemption was purchased with the precious blood of Jesus (1 Peter 1:18-19). Despite the lies Satan sows in the earthly realm to hinder our flow of power, believers must be confident that Jesus is our overflowing power supply.

Reconciliation and Peace

Another essential impact of the blood of Jesus is reconciliation. Just to remind you, sin separates man from God and produces God's anger against the wicked everyday (Psalm 7:11). Through the reconciliation of the blood, there is a position shift. No longer are we strangers far away. The blood of Jesus gives us access to God by destroying the dividing wall of isolation reconciling us to Him. Now, all persons who believe are members of the family and kingdom of God.

And having made peace through the blood of his cross, by him to reconcile all things unto himself; by him, I say, whether they be things in earth, or things in heaven. And you, that were sometimes alienated and enemies in your mind by wicked works, yet now hath he reconciled (Colossians 1:20-21).

But now in Christ Jesus ye who sometimes were far off are made nigh by the blood of Christ. For he is our peace, who hath made both one, and hath broken down the middle wall of partition between us (Ephesians 2:13-14).

For believers, the reconciliation component of the blood is important when Satan attempts to attack us with the spirit of fear to cripple the operation of spiritual warfare against him. Believers being tormented in their minds by fear are robbed of peace. Satan attempts to convince them they are weak and incapable to function in the operations of the Holy Spirit and the power of the blood. In addition, Satan also attempts to convince believers that God is not present to rescue or deliver them from that torment. The blood coupled with the Word cleanses believers' minds from the wicked works of Satan. Furthermore, peace came through the blood of Jesus and is an attribute of reconciliation.

Jesus as our peace renders God's presence removing fear and releasing boldness for believers to operate in the power of the blood. Embracing this boldness empowers believers to take authority over the works of Satan pleading the blood. How powerful is pleading the blood in the mouth of a true believer? It is extremely powerful. Demons tremble every time a believer pleas the blood of Jesus against them because the blood has prevailing power.

The blood of Jesus Covers

Satan and the kingdom of darkness cannot penetrate the blood that covers every believer and everything connected to them. When Satan sees the blood on believers lives, he sees the blood seal with a stamp stating, "NO ACCESS PASS OVER." An example of this action is in the book of Exodus. God was releasing the children of Israel from the bondage of their enemies, the Egyptians. After Moses made several requests to leave and received oppositional warfare from Pharaoh, God performed signs to show Pharaoh His judgment and power to rescue His people. Before the final judgment against Egypt, Israel completed the feast and offering of the Passover Lamb, God instructs Moses regarding the purpose of the blood to prepare Israel for a mass exodus out of Egypt.

> *And ye shall take a bunch of hyssop, and dip it in the blood that is in the bason, and strike the lintel and the two side post with the blood that is in the bason; and none of you shall go out at the door of his house until the morning. For the Lord will pass through to smite the Egyptians; and when he seeth the blood upon the lintel, and on the two side posts, the Lord will pass over the door, and will not suffer the destroyer to come in unto your houses to smite you (Exodus 12:22-23).*

Take note that Moses gave the children of Israel explicit instructions regarding applying the blood of the Passover Lamb. Specifically, the children of Israel were to apply the blood to the top of the door and on both sides, and stay in the house. Their obedience in applying the blood would allow the Lord to protect them from the judgment of the death of the firstborn meant only for the Egyptians and the destroyer would not touch them. Exodus 12:28-29 states that God did exactly what He proclaimed releasing judgment on the Egyptians. From Pharaoh's house to the prison and the animals, the first born died.

And the children of Israel went away, and did as the Lord had commanded Moses and Aaron, so did they. And it came to pass, that at midnight the Lord smote all the firstborn in the land of Egypt, from the firstborn of Pharaoh that sat on his throne unto the firstborn of the captive that was in the dungeon; and all the firstborn of cattle.

As we examine the text, believers should pay close attention to what the destroyer was permitted to perform. The destroyer had permission to touch those uncovered by the blood. However, the destroyer did not penetrate the houses of the children of Israel that were fully covered nor the people who remained in their houses. In John chapter ten, Jesus gives insight to the destroyer who was not given permission to touch the children of Israel then or the believers now. In John 10:10a (AMP Version) Jesus states, "The thief comes only in order to steal and kill and destroy." Who is this thief Jesus mentions exposing his assignment? Satan. Therefore, the destroyer is also Satan, not God. God permitted the spirit of death to destroy the lives of the firstborn in Egypt, but the Lord's Passover Sacrifice was a protective shield to the children of Israel.

Someone may be saying how does this relate to believers today in spiritual warfare? In the same manner the blood related to Israel, the covering of the blood relates to us. As believers, we must employ the same principles of obedience as Israel in applying the blood. Satan, the destroyer is a real enemy. The blessing for believers is Jesus has revealed that He is the Door to salvation and is our Passover Lamb for the New Testament (John 10:9, 1 Corinthians 5:7, 1 Peter 1:19).

When spiritual warfare becomes intense for believers, we have to remain behind the Door and in a spiritual house. The blood covering is behind and in Jesus, the Door. Satan often attempts to draw believers outside the house and from Jesus the Door because he does not have access to destroy as long as believers are under the blood.

Even as Israel applied the blood on every critical point to protect them, it is critical that believers apply the blood against Satan's kingdom of darkness and over everything God has given us. Israel had the physical blood to apply as a covering only to the outside of the door. However, believers house the blood covenant and the Passover Lamb in our hearts covering us inside out and are given authority to proclaim the blood that saturates our being.

Revelation 12:11a states, "and they overcame him (Satan) by the blood of the Lamb." Every believer who partakes in Holy Communion partakes in the blood of the Passover Lamb (Matthew 26:17-28). This makes the blood a relevant continuum in our lives. Therefore, every believer who understands the relevance of the blood of Jesus will flow in the power of proclamation application in spiritual warfare. What does that mean? It means that pleading and applying the blood is done without hesitation or as an automatic action against Satan to those who accept the authority.

For example, when Satan attempts to attack your destiny, home, family, job, etc., believers begin proclaiming the blood in spiritual warfare coupled with the weapons of prayer and the name of Jesus. Armed with knowing there is overcoming power in the blood of Jesus that continues to prevail against the power of Satan, believers are victorious in the warfare.

Someone may say this is new to me and ask, "How do I operate in pleading the blood weapon against Satan?" Here are a few examples of proclamation application employing the blood of Jesus:

Satan in the name of Jesus I plea the blood of Jesus against every demonic attack, your works, activities, agenda, and cohorts, in every situation, conversation, and circumstance the blood of Jesus prevails.

In Jesus' name, I plea the blood against everything and everyone who attempts to block or hinder me, my spouse, my children, or family's destiny and purpose.

Father, in the name of Jesus, I ask that you cover myself, my husband/wife, children, family down to the babies, and church family in the blood of Jesus. Jesus, let your blood permeate, saturate, and penetrate our beings prevailing against Satan and his cohorts.

Cover my home every ceiling, window, wall, door, room, and everything in those rooms in the blood of Jesus. Cover the vehicles that are parked and that my family and I may ride or drive in the blood of Jesus. Assign your warring angels to assist us and give them charge over us. Bind accidents over the dangerous highways and byways and loose your divine protection and safety. Let us make it to every destination and return home safe in the name of Jesus.

Lord, rebuke thieves and robbers and vandals and do not let them come near my person, property, family, identity, or anything that pertains to me. Let the blood of Jesus prevail against them and give your strong fighting/warring angels charge concerning us to protect us from all hurt harm, danger, evil seen and unseen in Jesus name. If anyone attempts to harm us in any way open their eyes to see the angels surrounding us that fear and dread will come upon them. If they continue their pursuit to hurt or harm us sexually or physically in anyway, let them drop dead where they stand in the name of Jesus.

Father, in the name of Jesus, I plea the blood against every strategist and strategy of Satan and his cohorts on my job and place of employment, at my children's' school, in the local church assembly, and every arena we occupy. The blood prevails against every hidden meeting or counsel that attempts to rise against me. I cancel every verbal and written agenda, for the blood of Jesus prevails destroying every work.

In the name of Jesus, I decree unprecedented divine favor in the eyes of all from the least to the greatest in every situation, conversation, matter, and circumstance.

Hopefully, the above examples have encouraged you to make the decision today to utilize the blood weapon with confidence because the blood of Jesus still works!

Chapter Four Review

1. Why does the blood of Jesus have a great impact in spiritual warfare?

2. Was the ordinance of atonement a permanent solution for sin?

3. Did God only want atone our sins?

4. Did the blood of animals have the power to accomplish the goal?

5. Who was the only person qualified to fulfill God's desire?

6. Why is the history of the blood so important?

7. What happens when believers have faith in the power of the blood of Jesus?

8. What does Satan see on the believer?

9. Why is the untouchable component powerful?

10. What is the sin eraseability power of the blood of Jesus?

11. Why should we praise God that the blood of Jesus is sufficient for our sins?

12. Why does Satan NOT want believers to understand about the completed work of the blood of Jesus?

13. Through the blood of Jesus, what does redemption accomplish?

14. How was redemption purchased?

15. What happens through the reconciliation of the blood?

16. Why does Satan attempt to cripple believers with fear in the reconciliation component?

17. How does Jesus remove fear?

_____

_____

18. How powerful is pleading the blood of Jesus in the life of a true believer?

_____

_____

19. What does Satan see on the believers' blood seal stamp?

_____

_____

20. Who is the destroyer and the thief?

_____

21. Who was the Lord to the nation of Israel?

_____

22. Who is Jesus for the New Testament believers?

_____

23. Where should believers be in the midst of intense spiritual warfare?

_____

_____

24. What happens when believers understand the revelation of the blood of Jesus?

___

___

25. What does Revelation 12:11 say?

___

___

Chapter Five

The Weapon of the Praise

And when he had consulted with the people, he appointed singers unto the Lord, and that should praise the beauty of holiness, as they went out before the army, and to say, Praise the Lord, for his mercy endureth for ever. And when they began to sing and to praise, the Lord set ambushments against the children of Ammon, Moab, and mount Seir, which were come against Judah; and they were smitten (2 Chronicles 20:21-22).

In the kingdom of God, praise is necessary and a powerful weapon in spiritual warfare. Among the local bodies of the kingdom of God, Satan attempts to convince church leaders and believers that praise is not necessary. To them, quiet worship is preferred over the loud noise of psalmists, dancing, and lively music. Satan lies stating God does not need all these theatrics to move in a service. Furthermore, Satan may try to convince believers that any praise is accepted because it all comes from God. This statement is a lie from the pit of hell. Any praise that does not magnify God is not from God.

Satan knows there is power in praise. Being a former anointed praise cherub of God, Satan lost his opportunity and privilege to be saturated in God's presence (Ezekiel 28: 13-17). Therefore, he attempts to distort pure praise. From his kingdom of darkness, Satan produces praise music and songs that are sensual praising idols and the works of the flesh. When believers participate in Satan's type of praise, they care more about the things of this world or their fleshly desires. In essence, they are not in pursuit after the things that are totally pleasing to God. In the Word of God, this type of believer is considered carnal or a person who operates according to the desires of his/her flesh. However, the Word of God reveals that the flesh is an enemy to God and anyone who dwells in the things of the flesh fulfilling his/her worldly desires cannot please God (Romans 8:6-9).

Nevertheless, Satan attempts to convince believers his praise is innocent and "music is music." This is a deception perpetrated by Satan to hinder the believer's ability to war through his access in his/her life in the area of polluted praise disguised as "innocent music." The truth is God is holy and does not accept Satan's sensual praise. Satan's praise is unholy and impure, and does not give the glory to God.

With that being said, the profound reality is that the eternal purpose for praise is a matter of reverence unto God. Since God created us to praise Him, loving pure praise should be a natural attribute for believers (Psalm 147:1). Dwelling in God's presence is a personal benefit that empowers believers. In the midst of the praise solely given to God, believers attract and capture God's attention for Him to reside in our lives and concerns.

In Psalm 150, David encourages praise unto God to flow from the sanctuary. He informs us that we should praise God for who He is, what He has done, for His excellent greatness, and with instruments. The last verse states that everything that has breath should praise God.

While it is true that everything that has breath can praise God, only anointed praise births strength to immobilize Satan's attacks (Psalm 8:2). In addition, only anointed praisers who are pure consecrated vessels of God have the ability to war in the spirit realm. When anointed praisers war with pure worship and praise unto God, they enter the heavenly realm combating the unseen demonic activity in the atmosphere shifting the atmosphere. As consecrated anointed psalmists and musicians, they have the ability to drive devils out of the atmosphere. This action is demonstrated by King David. King David was an anointed psalmist and musician. The Bible declares that King David played his harp and drove out the devil that was tormenting King Saul refreshing his spirit (1 Samuel 16:23).

Today, when anointed psalmists and musicians use the instruments of their voices and musical instruments to shift the atmosphere in the houses of worship, their praise makes it conducive for God to move mightily yielding the way for ministers of the Word to go forth without opposition. If pure praise stops demonic activity in the houses of worship, this type of praise will also effectively shift any atmosphere of a true believer in the midst of spiritual warfare. The Word of God reveals the effectiveness of praise in spiritual warfare by explaining how the nation of Israel, Joshua, and Jehoshaphat sent Judah first; how the spirit of heaviness is destroyed by praise; and how Paul and Silas opened prison doors with praise.

Send Judah First: the Meaning and Characteristic of Praise

According to Judges chapters nineteen-twenty, certain men from tribe of Benjamin raped and murdered a concubine. The husband was outraged and requested justice. When an inquiry was done and the

Israelites requested the Benjamites to hand over the men that committed the crime, they unapologetically would not and provoked a civil war in Israel uniting eleven tribes against one tribe. After gathering their men of war together, the united Israelites went to the house of God seeking instruction regarding the battle. The Israelites wanted to know who should lead the battle.

The Israelites arose and went up to the house of God (Bethel) and asked counsel of God and said, Which of us shall take the lead to battle against the Benjamites? And the Lord said, Judah shall go up first (Judges 20:18, AMP Version).

Notice that God said send Judah first before the battle. The question comes to mind, why did God say send Judah first? For clarity, let's look at the book of Genesis to review Judah's meaning and characteristics.

Genesis Chapter 29:35 gives an account to the birth of Judah, Jacob and Leah's third son. What makes Judah interesting is the significance of his name. Leah stated, "Now, will I praise the Lord" signifying that Judah's name means praise. Later, Jacob pronouncing blessings on his sons prophetically before he died spoke to Judah.

Judah, you are the one whom your brothers shall praise; your hand shall be on the neck of your enemies; your father's sons shall bow down to you. Judah, a lion's cub! With the prey my son, you have gone high up the mountain. He stooped down, he crouched like a lion, and like a lioness–who dares provoke and rouse him? The scepter or leadership shall not depart from Judah, nor the ruler's staff from between his feet, until Shiloh (the Messiah, the Peaceful One) comes to Whom it belongs, and to Him shall be the obedience of the people (Genesis 49:8-10, AMP Version)

Jacob prophetically proclaimed a blessing on Judah and with the blessing came an anointing of empowerment. Judah has preference among his brethren. Judah will not be prey, but is anointed to destroy his enemy. Judah is anointed with the strength and essence of a lion. The essence of the lion is king or leader. Judah will lead to carry the rod to bring order, the Word, and great warrior leaders including King Jesus will be a part of his ancestry. Having said that, remember Judah means praise. After reviewing the prophetic characteristics of the tribe of praise, it is evident why God sent Judah before the battle to lead the way.

Based on Jacob's natural proclamation, supernaturally the anointing of praise goes first and believers will not be the prey of Satan and the kingdom of darkness. However, praise will choke the enemy, his cohorts, and their agenda. When believers embrace praise as a weapon, praise will produce anointed strength without fear within us. The reason why is because Jesus our King and Anointed one, the Lion of Judah (praise) abides and His Spirit ushers us into His presence.

Praise sees Satan's plots in high places. Therefore, provoking anointed praise attacks every agenda of darkness making the enemy subject to God's presence. Believers, we must send Judah first. Anointed praise equipped with power does an effective work against the kingdom of darkness.

The Ram's horn trumpet and a Shout

Two examples that demonstrates the effectiveness of praise going before the battle is Joshua 6:2-5 and 2 Chronicles 20:21-24. In Joshua chapter six, God gave Joshua instructions how he should enter the city of Jericho. Jericho was given to Israel as a possession. The problem was Jericho was a city fortified with high walls. The children of Israel could not just march in or initially employ natural weapons to capture the city. Therefore, the primary weapon God provided for them to go into the battle with was the weapon of praise. After some Spirit-led walking around, God gave Joshua the supernatural method of a ram's horn trumpet and a shout. Joshua 6:2-5, 15-16 (AMP Version) reveals the method given to Joshua.

> *And the Lord said unto Joshua, See, I have given Jericho, its king and mighty men of valor, in your hands. You shall march around the enclosure, all the men of war going around the city once. This you shall do for six days (2-3).*

> *And seven priests shall bear before the ark seven trumpets of rams' horns; and on the seventh day you shall march around the enclosure seven times, and the priests shall blow the trumpets (4).*

> *When they make a long blast with the ram's horn and you hear the sound of the trumpet, all the people shall shout with a great shout; and the wall of the enclosure shall fall down in its place and the people shall go up over it, every man straight before him (5).*

On the seventh day they rose early at daybreak and marched around the city as usual, only on that day they compassed the city seven times. And the seventh time, when the priests had blown the trumpets, Joshua said to the people, Shout! For the Lord has given you the city (15-16).

It was very important that Joshua obeyed God's instructions completely to have the final results. Although Jericho walls appeared as a stumbling block, Israel had to continue to go forward in a Spirit-led march around the stumbling block to get to where God was taking them and to possess what God had promised. Furthermore, even though there were armed men assigned to protect the priests, the priests were consecrated vessels surrounding God's presence represented by the ark. With the weapons of ram's horn trumpets, the priests' assignment was vital because they had to sound the alarm in the midst of the battle.

By applying the weapons of praise of ram's horns and a shout, God declared to Joshua the enemy and the walls would fall before Israel. The ram's horns long blast alarms the enemy that the battle is commencing shifting the atmosphere and the shout proclaims Israel's victory in advance. Together the weapons of praise shook the fortified walls at their foundation causing them to crumble before Israel. Sending praise first was effective!

Even as the weapon of praise rendered victory to Israel, it will do the same for believers. Believers of God faced with oppositions or fortified walls must continue to be led by the Spirit of God and move forward. Although it may appear as if you are going in circles, or taking a while to obtain what God has already given, the important thing to remember is the outcome in God is victory. With this knowledge, sound the alarm of anointed praise to remind Satan that God is present in your praise and you will possess every promise God has given you. Shout unto God with a voice of triumph and watch fortified walls completely crumble and every demonic stumbling block destroyed.

Send Anointed Praisers and God will fight the Battle

What do leaders of praise do when Satan attempts to send a full arsenal against them because they are re-establishing the standards of God connected to the very heart of praise? In 2 Chronicles 20, there was a multitude of enemies who had combined their powers waging war against the tribe of praise (Judah). King Jehoshaphat's first step was to seek the

Lord for direction. Not long after, God prophetically spoke through Jahaziel to tell Judah, "Be not afraid nor dismayed by reason of this great multitude; for the battle is not yours, but God's." In other words, God is going to fight this battle for Judah.

The mention of Jahaziel as the vessel of God and his lineage to Asaph is significant. The reason why is because Asaph was one of the three appointed praise leaders of King David and a composer. There were one hundred and twenty-eight singers of Asaph (Ezra 2:41, I Chronicles 15:17). As Levites in the temple, his family ministered in the presence of God in the ministry of music (I Chronicles 16:5). In addition, they were anointed to prophesy and prophesied freely by the order of King David (I Chronicles 25:2). Therefore, Jahaziel's life as a true man of God and prophetic praiser was relevant to the reception of the prophetic word. King Jehoshaphat believed God and was encouraged by the answered prayer. Receiving God's plans, King Jehoshaphat encourages the people of praise to believe God and His prophet.

What is the plan against this multitude of enemies? Employ the weapon of praise. King Jehoshaphat sent Judah first. In 2 Chronicles

20:21-22, which is the opening scripture of this chapter, King Jehoshaphat "appointed singers to sing to the Lord and praise Him in their holy priestly garments as they went out before the army." He appointed anointed praisers in right standing with God to lead the tribe of praise with resounding praise of thanksgiving saturating their atmosphere with the presence of God.

This praise caused God Himself to step in the midst of the multitude of enemies and their traps. God confounded them positioning them to ambush each other (v.22). Losing trust in their alliance, the enemies "all helped to destroy one another" and all Judah (praise) witnessed were dead bodies. Not one enemy was left standing (2 Chronicles 20:23-24).

Hallelujah! When Satan attempts to surround believers of God with astronomical situations or circumstances and demonic aggression from every direction, praise is the weapon to employ. Give God the glory in advance. God Himself will rest in the midst of holy praise that magnifies His name. In the same way that God fought for King

Jehoshaphat who dwelled in praise, He will fight for every believer that does the same.

Praise Destroys the Spirit of Heaviness

Praise is equipped to destroy the bondage of heaviness. Heaviness is a spirit that produces overwhelming feelings of depression and oppression that will hinder purpose robbing hope and virtue from the lives of believers. The good news is believers do not have to be bound to the spirit of heaviness.

> *To appoint unto them that mourn in Zion, to give unto them beauty for ashes, the oil of joy for mourning, the garment of praise for the spirit of heaviness (Isaiah 61:3a).*

God has given believers the weapon of praise as a mantle covering us. Satan's purpose is to make believers succumb to the spirit of heaviness. He attempts to attack their minds with feelings of anxiety, depression, oppression, defeat, and hopelessness. Satan will say there is no reason to praise God; however, anointed believers will yet praise God. The reason why believers are resilient in praise is because we understand that in the presence of God there is fullness of joy (Psalm 16:11).

Even with tears flowing and a heart with questions, anointed praisers do not respond to what we feel or what is seen, but what is known about our God. There arises an assurance that God will intervene and turn everything around. Therefore, instead of subsiding to Satan's purpose, anointed praisers do the opposite exalting God with singing, dancing, and thanksgiving in the face of the attack. This very action of praise confuses Satan and cancels his purpose making the mantle of praise a powerful weapon against the spirit of heaviness.

Praise Opens Prison Doors

The Apostles Paul and Silas understood effectual praise in spiritual warfare. While in the city of Philippi on a missionary journey, Paul encounters a young lady demonically influenced by the spirit of witchcraft and divination and casted the devil out of her. The people that made money from her practices pressed charges against Paul and Silas. They were falsely accused, tried, openly beaten, and tossed into prison. In addition, stocks were placed on their feet and the jailor had to watch them carefully. However, in their darkest hour, Acts chapter sixteen explains how Paul and Silas created an atmosphere of praise unto God in prison.

And at midnight Paul and Silas prayed, and sang praises unto God: and the prisoners heard them. And suddenly there was a great earthquake, so that the foundations of the prison were shaken: and immediately all the doors were opened, and every one's bands were loosed (Acts 16:25-26).

Even though they were mistreated and falsely arrested, they still had a song of praise. The sincerity of their praise captured God's attention provoking Him to move even in the prison. The earthquake moved suddenly breaking up what imprisoned them. At the same time, doors were opened immediately loosing those in proximity to embrace the move of God. One person captivated was the jailor. Bearing witness to the mighty move of God, he was introduced to the God of Paul and Silas. Praise was the weapon that opened the door for the salvation of the jailor's house.

For this cause, believers cannot be silent or withdraw the weapon of praise. There are non-believers who need anointed praisers experiencing a midnight season, but has power in praise that will cancel the assignment of Satan's prison. The non-believers will take notice and witness a real move of God that will penetrate their heart to salvation. In turn, God will make Himself known by shaking the foundation of everything that held them captive, set them free, and open new doors of grace and success.

Believers of God, it is imperative that we understand that praise is a true weapon. God desires believers to wear holy garments of praise making this weapon effective against the kingdom of darkness. If you are a believer who has not tapped into the realm of praise, now is the time. Do not allow Satan to convince you to compromise pure praise that renders glory to God. Make up in your mind that your mouth shall praise the Lord (Psalms 63.3, 145:21). Remember, the more you praise God, the more He will live in your praises.

Here are a few proclamations to assist beginners to the weapon of praise and encourage those already functioning in anointed praise that will counter the attacks of Satan:

Lord, I thank you; bless your name Lord; I love you Lord; You are wonderful, magnificent, and marvelous; Lord you are awesome and mighty; You are a giant God: Thank you for being my Father, You are the best Father ever; There is no Dad like my Heavenly Father; Thank you Jesus for being my Lord, Savior, big brother, and best friend; Thank you Holy Spirit for being my Helper and best friend; Thank you Jesus for giving me your love, joy, hope, and peace; Lord, You are great and greatly to be praised; God, you are the only God who is holy; Your mercies endures forever; God, you are a greater than any situation or circumstance; there is none who can stand against or before my God! You alone are God and there is none other than you; Thank you for being my provider and supplying every need; Thank you for being my healer and the healer of all who believe; You are sovereign and control all things; I thank you that you will make a way out of no way; I trust you Lord, my times are in your hand; Satan is defeated and my God is exalted; Thank you for being a God who answers prayers and keeps His promises; Thank you that you are greater in me that he that is in this world; Thank you that I can do all things through Jesus who strengthens me: Thank you Lord for arising and scattering every enemy! Through You Jesus I am more than a conqueror and victorious; I shall make a boast in the Lord: I exalted You God above all and everything; Thank you Jesus for new mercy, grace and Your compassions failing not; Praises be unto You Lord for your mercies shall endure forever.

Eventually, you will effectively apply praise in every situation becoming skilled and anointed wearing the weapon of praise as a precious garment of power.

Weapons for Spiritual Warfare | The Weapon of Praise

Chapter Five Review

1. What is the lie Satan makes about music?

___

___

2. Why does Satan attempt to distort pure praise?

___

___

___

3. Are you anointed to shift the atmosphere and drive out devils?

___

___

4. How did King David shift King Saul's atmosphere?

___

5. Why did God send Judah first?

___

___

6. What does the name Judah mean?

___

Weapons for Spiritual Warfare					The Weapon of Praise

7. What came with blessing in Judah?

_____

_____

8. If praise goes before a believer, what happens?

_____

_____

9. What does praise see and attack?

_____

_____

10. What was the supernatural method given to Joshua for battle?

_____

_____

11. What type of march did Israel move in?

_____

12. What did the priest do?

_____

13. What was the impact of the weapon of praise?

_____

_____

14. The weapons of praise gave the nation of Israel victory over their enemies. Does the weapon of praise work for believers the same way?

15. What was King Jehoshaphat first step?

16. Who is Jahaziel?

17. Who did Jehoshaphat appoint to lead the battle?

18. Who stepped in the multitude of the enemies?

19. What happened to the enemies?

Weapons for Spiritual Warfare   The Weapon of Praise

20. What should believers do when we are surrounded by astronomical situations and demonic aggression?

_____

_____

21. What is heaviness?

_____

_____

22. What does Isaiah 61:3 say?

_____

_____

_____

23. What is the weapon of praise to believers?

_____

24. What does praise do to Satan?

_____

_____

25. After being mistreated and falsely arrested, what did Paul and Silas do in prison?

_____

_____

26. What does anointed praise do for the non-believers?

_____

_____

Chapter Six

The Weapon of Fasting

Is not this the fast that I have chosen? To loose the bands of wickedness, to undo the heavy burdens, and to let the oppressed go free, and that ye break every yoke? (Isaiah 58:6).

Fasting is a powerful weapon in the lives of the believers and against the kingdom of darkness. Fasting requires discipline and believers with a consistent fast life fortify precise execution of the weapon with authority. What is fasting? Fasting is abstaining from food and sometimes water.[13] Usually, fasting is combined with the weapon of prayer. Depending on the believer's desire and the leading of the Holy Spirit, the fast may last for an hour, hours, a day and a night, days and nights, a week, or weeks. The purpose of fasting is to afflict or humble the soul as a personal sacrifice of obedience in the presence of God bringing the body or flesh under subjection or control to the Holy Spirit. He, the Holy Spirit, is given permission to reign and govern rendering a desire for believers to feast on the Word of God, which flows strength to the inner

---

[13] Unger, (Chicago, Moody Press, 1977), 345, s.v. "fasting."

man of the Spirit. What makes fasting such a powerful weapon in spiritual warfare is that the flesh is weak from the lack of food, but the Spirit is strong from the lack of the reign of the flesh. When fasting is done properly, believers are sensitive to the leading of the Holy Spirit, given revelation knowledge and discernment, granted favor, and flow in authority destroying every yoke of the enemy.

The Word of God teaches believers that there is a proper and improper way to fast. In Isaiah chapter fifty-eight and Matthew chapter six, God expresses how important fasting is to Him and why fasting must be done properly. For the nation of Israel, fasting was vital and usually combined with prayer. In times of calamity, men and women of God in Israel would humble themselves in fasting to seek direction, to have victory in battle against enemies, to repent for sins, and wait for God to hear and answer them (I Samuel 7: 1-8). As Israel grew as a nation, they continued to fast; however, fasting became more of a ritual and without sincere humility. Furthermore, their motives for fasting changed causing God to render a deaf ear to their cry.

The Improper Way to Fast

In Isaiah chapter fifty-eight, Israel was seeking God's assistance and did what they were accustomed to do as a nation: fast and pray. However, their fast offering was an insincere and unholy sacrifice to God because they had not turned from the sins that displeased God. Yet, they expected God to move on their behalf. When God did not respond, His people questioned why God did not see and honor their fasting. The Prophet Isaiah addresses the issue in Isaiah 58: 3-5 (AMP Version).

> *Why have we fasted, they say, and You do not see it? Why have we afflicted ourselves, and You take no knowledge of it? Behold O Israel, on the day of your fast when you should be grieving for your sins, you find profit in your business, and (instead of stopping all work, as the law implies you and your workmen should do) you extort from your hired servants a full amount of labor (3).*

> *The facts are that you fast only for strife and debate and to smite with the fist of wickedness. Fasting as you do today will not cause your voice to be heard on high (4).*

Is such a fast as yours what I have chosen, a day for a man to humble himself with sorrow in his soul? Is true fasting merely mechanical? Is it only to bow down his head like a bulrush and to spread sackcloth and ashes under him to indicate a condition of heart that he does not have? Will you call this a fast and an acceptable day to the Lord? (5)

According to God, He did not hear Israel or honor the fast because it was done improperly. Israel continued business as usual fasting for strife without a sincere heart of humility. Their fast was a mere form of religious ritual and was hypocritical. Knowing the motives of their hearts and their sinful behaviors, God did not accept the fast.

In the same fashion as Isaiah, Jesus addresses the improper way to fast specifying the motives regarding public appearance when fasting.

Moreover when ye fast, be not as the hypocrites, of a sad countenance: for they disfigure their faces that they may appear unto men to fast. Verily I say unto you, they have their reward (Matthew 6:16).

According to Jesus, fasting should be done in secret and evident only to God. In times past, garments of sackcloth and ashes on the forehead were symbols of the men or women of God humbling themselves before God and man in fasting (Nehemiah 9:1).

Even though fasting is an act of humility before God, Jesus considers an outer display of humility as a means to gain attention and a hypocritical act for the empathy of men. Therefore, believers who fast bringing attention to themselves for the pity of men to tell them how noble or an awesome job they have done have wrong motives and lose the reward. The reward is the outcome the fast should produce from God. Therefore, fasting done improperly exposes the motive of the heart yielding zero results from God.

The Proper Way to Fast

Differing from the improper fast, fasting done properly is beneficial and pleasing to God. As believers, knowing the proper way to fast empowers believers to comprise fasting as a vital element in our spiritual lives. In Matthew chapter six, Jesus conveys the proper way to capture God's attention through fasting and instructs the proper way to begin the fast.

But thou, when thou fastest, anoint thine head, and wash thy face; That thou appear not unto men to fast, but thy Father, which is in secret: and thy Father, which seeth in secret, shall reward thee openly (Matthew 6: 17-18).

After believers have sought God regarding fasting or have been led by the Holy Spirit to fast, Jesus teaches the first step to begin a fast is the anointing. The act of anointing our head with oil is a symbol of being set apart unto God for fasting and being empowered by His grace to perform and complete the task.

Contrary to the past public display of sackcloth and ashes, Jesus teaches that believers should wash the anointing oil off by washing our faces. The reason why this is important is to ensure that our fast is not on public display, but seen only by God. With this private showing to God, comes a public reward from God. This is essential because Jesus is making believers aware that fasting done properly is never in vain; however, it is purposeful with the intention of receiving manifested results.

What exactly are the results and benefits that are produced from fasting properly? Isaiah chapter fifty-eight explains in detail the fast that makes God happy and the benefits released to believers (Isaiah 58:6-11 (AMP Version).

> *Rather is not this the fast I have chosen: to loose the bonds of wickedness, to undo the bands of the yoke, to let the oppressed go free, and that you break every enslaving yoke? Is it not to divide your bread with the hungry and bring the homeless poor into your house–when you see the naked, that you cover him, and that you hide not yourself from the needs of your own flesh and blood? (6-7)*

> *Then shall your light break forth like the morning, and your healing (your restoration and the power of a new life) shall spring forth speedily; your righteousness (your rightness, your justice, and your right relationship with God) shall go before you conducting you to peace and prosperity and the glory of the Lord shall be your rear guard (8).*

> *Then you shall call, and the Lord will answer; you shall cry, and He will say, Here I am. If you take away from your midst yokes of oppression*

wherever you find them, the finger pointed in scorn toward the oppressed or the godly, and every form of false, harsh, unjust, and wicked speaking

And if you pour out that with which you sustain your own life for the hungry and satisfy the need of the afflicted, then shall your light rise in darkness, and your obscurity and gloom become like the noonday (9-10).

And the Lord shall guide you continually and satisfy you in drought and in dry places and make strong your bones. And you shall be like a watered garden and like a spring of water whose water fail not (11).

According to Isaiah, the proper fast that makes God happy is the fast that is on assignment discerning needs to benefit others. Yes, believers may fast for personal things. However, what makes God's fast so marvelous is that while believers are interceding on the behalf of and assisting others, God renders blessings for our sacrifice. These blessings entail open revelation, healing, restoration, a relationship with God in right standing, overflowing new life, favor, peace, and God's glory rests heavily upon the believer's life. In addition, believers will have the ear of God to answer every prayer and there is an overflow of the Holy Spirit giving direction in every situation. Because of a simple act of obedience to God, He opens the windows of heaven with great rewards.

Fasting as a Weapon in Spiritual Warfare

In Isaiah chapter fifty-eight, God makes believers aware that fasting has a purpose. This purpose is spiritual warfare. God's chosen fast is a fast that will "loose the bonds of wickedness" and "destroy yokes" that the oppressed become free and delivered. Satan attempts to oppress some believers or hold those dear to them hostage to habits, relationships, situations, or demonic influences of darkness that possess and control their lives. Through the weapon of fasting combined with the weapon of prayer, every "enslaving yoke" is destroyed and freedom is a reality in the lives of believers and sinners. This is evident in Matthew chapter seventeen when a father requested his son's freedom from demonic control. In Matthew 17: 14-21 (AMP Version), Jesus explains that fasting and prayer were the principal weapons needed for the boy's situation.

And when they approached the multitude, a man came up to Him, kneeling before Him and saying, Lord, do pity and have mercy on my son for he has epilepsy (is moonstruck) and he suffers terribly; for frequently he falls into the fire and many times into the water. And I brought him to Your disciples, and they were not able to cure him (14-16).

And Jesus answered, O you unbelieving (warped, wayward, rebellious) and thoroughly perverse generation! How long am I to remain with you? How long am I to bear with you? Bring him here to Me. And Jesus rebuked the demon, and it came out of him, and the boy was cured instantly (17-18).

Then the disciples came to Jesus and asked privately, Why could we not drive it out? He said to them, Because of the littleness of your faith (that is, your lack of firmly relying trust). For truly I say to you, if you have faith that is living like a grain of mustard seed, you can say to this mountain, move from here to yonder place, and it will move; nothing will be impossible to you. But this kind does not go out except by prayer and fasting (19-21).

In the midst of many, this father captures the attention of Jesus. He humbles himself before Jesus seeking deliverance for his son who is demon possessed. The spirit in operation is the infirmity named epilepsy. This demon attempted to kill the boy. The father explains to Jesus that the disciples could not help him. In his response, Jesus created an atmosphere of faith by rebuking doubt and giving understanding how a lack of faith will hinder the move of God in the lives of believers and the lives of those we are attempting to assist. In addition, Jesus gave the minimum requirement for great faith and he cast the devil out of the boy.

How does this connect to fasting? Soon after, the disciples wanted to understand why the demon did not respond to them. Jesus reveals this assignment requires faith combined with fasting and prayer. Without fasting, some demonic influences will not be penetrated and destroyed. The demon of epilepsy had been in that child's life since birth and had gained serious ground in his life with an assignment to kill him. In other words, the demon was strong and stubborn. For this reason, Jesus emphasized with faith, "this kind does not go out except by fasting and prayer."

As believers, there may be some habits or situations that have been in your life or in the life of your loved ones that has been there for a longtime and has gained ground in your lives. Satan has convinced you that nothing can be done or no one can assist you or your loved ones to release and remove the demonic grip filling your hearts with fear and doubt. Satan states accepting this habit, state, or situation is natural part of your life. Satan is a liar! For stubborn situations, habits, and spirits, Jesus encourages fasting and prayer. Satan may appear like he has the upper hand, but God has already decreed victory in Jesus. A fast done properly will penetrate the powers of darkness and destroy every yoke. Satan and his cohorts' assignments will be canceled in the situations, habits will be broken and destroyed, and spirits are evicted out of the lives of your loved ones and atmospheres.

When Satan attempts to send opposition on every side, fasting is the answer. God will give directions for victory. King Jehoshaphat had enemies coming from every direction to fight him. He sought the Lord in fasting and prayer.

Then there came some that told Jehoshaphat, saying, there cometh a great multitude against thee from beyond the sea on this side Syria; and behold, they be in Hazazon-tamar, which is Engedi. And Jehoshaphat feared, and set himself to seek the Lord, and proclaimed a fast throughout all Judah (2 Chronicles 20:2-3).

Notice that the thought of so many enemies warring against King Jehoshaphat gave space to the spirit of fear. Fortunately, King Jehoshaphat's faith in God superseded fear compelling him to position himself and the nation for battle applying the weapons of fasting and prayer. God gave King Jehoshaphat a sure word of direction. Regardless of how many enemies gathered together against Judah, God declared He will personally destroy them.

Like Judah, fasting will fine tune the ears of believers to hear a sure word of direction and victory in overwhelming circumstances. Despite the different directions the enemy attempts to come, believers who humble themselves in fasting captures God's attention to intervene on our behalf.

Fasting against Personal and National Annihilation

In the same manner as King Jehoshaphat, Queen Esther understood how imperative the weapon of fasting was at the announcement of the annihilation of her people. As an agent of Satan, Haman convinced the king to sign a decree to kill and annihilate all the Jews young and old and sent letters throughout the provinces of Persia (Esther 3:13). After her uncle Mordecai made her aware of the detriment of herself and the Jews, Queen Esther encouraged the Jewish people and her maidens to fast with her. The purpose of the fast was for two reasons. According to Esther 4:16, 5:1-3 (AMP Version), the first reason was to have favor with the king because it was against the law for her to enter his presence without being summoned.

Go, gather together all the Jews that are present in Shushan, and fast for me; and neither eat nor drink for three days, night or day. I also and my maids will fast as you do. Then I will go to the king, though it is against the law; and if I perish, I perish (4:16).

On the third day of the fast Esther put on her royal robes and stood in the royal or inner court of the king's palace opposite his throne room. The king was sitting on his throne facing the main entrance of the palace (5:1).

And when the king saw Esther the queen standing in the court, she obtained favor in his sight, and he held out to her the golden scepter that was in his hand. So Esther drew near and touched the tip of the scepter. Then the king said to her, What will you have, Queen Esther? What is your request? It shall be given you, even to the half of the kingdom (5:2-3).

Fasting as the primary weapon of choice was beneficial for Queen Esther. After fasting for two days and nights, Queen Esther received a release on the third day to enter into the palace. While in the inner court, the king took notice of Queen Esther and granted her permission to enter his presence without repercussion granting her favor. Before she revealed her request to the king, he had already granted her request.

Believers of God, fasting thrusts us into the inner court of the King's presence. Even as Queen Esther found favor, believers warring in the spirit realm on the behalf of the kingdom of God are granted favor. God has promised to answer prayers in advance as a benefit for believers who fast sincerely. According to Psalm 91:15, believers can call upon God in trouble and He has promised to answer, deliver, and honor us.

After Queen Esther received the open reward of favor from the king, it cleared the way for the second reason for the fast. The second reason for Queen Esther's fast was to expose Haman and cancel the assignment of annihilation against the Jewish people. Due to the fast, Queen Esther received wisdom, direction, and patience for the detrimental situation. While she operated in obedience to the Spirit of God, God had the opportunity to divinely intervene changing the order of events in the spirit realm by the end of the third day of fasting. On that night, God moved on the king who was the only person with the authority in the earthly realm to change the plans against Mordecai, Queen Esther, and the Jews. While Haman hang gallows for Mordecai's demise (Esther 5:14), the Holy Spirit reminds the king about Mordecai saving his life. Furthermore, God made Mordecai's enemy decree favor and blessings upon him (Esther 6:1-3, 6, 8-11, AMP Version).

On that night the king could not sleep; and he ordered that the book of memorable deeds, the chronicles be brought, and they were read before the king. And it was found written there how Mordecai had told of Bigthana and Teresh, two of the king's attendants who guarded the door, who had sought to lay hands on King Ahasuerus. And the king said, What honor or distinction has been given Mordecai for this? Then the king's servants who ministered to him said, Nothing has been done for him (1-3).

So Haman came in. And the king said to him, What shall be done to the man whom the king delights to honor? Now Haman said to himself, to whom would the king delight to do honor more than to me? (6) Let royal apparel be brought which the king has worn and the horse which the king has ridden, and a royal crown be set on his head (8).

And let the apparel and the horse be delivered to the hand of one of the king's most noble princes. Let him array the man whom the king delights to honor, and conduct him on horseback through the open square of the city, and proclaim before him, thus shall it be done to the man whom the king delights to honor (9).

Then the king said to Haman, Make haste and take the apparel and the horse, as you have said, and do so to Mordecai the Jew, who sits at the king's gate. Leave out nothing that you have spoken (10).

> *Then Haman took the apparel and the horse and conducted Mordecai on horseback through the open square of the city, proclaiming before him, Thus shall it be done to the man whom the king delights to honor (11).*

Praise God! Satan's plans were foiled. God made Haman bless the very man he desired to kill. In addition, Mordecai's private fast produced open results of honor and exaltation from the king.

Instead of Haman's lies prospering in the kingdom regarding Mordecai, God renders public exposure of the truth from Haman's mouth to praise Mordecai the Jew. In the eyes of the kingdom, Haman had to serve his enemy and proclaim to the people that the king is not angry with Mordecai the Jew. On the contrary, Mordecai is a man "whom the king delights." This introduction of Mordecai reveals the power shift taking place in the heavenly realm for the Jews while in the earthly realm Haman's influence is shaken to humiliation.

Not long after God's intervention for Mordecai, Queen Esther exposes Haman to the king. Esther 7:3, 5-10 (AMP Version) records the event.

Then Queen Esther said, if I have found favor in your sight, O king and if it pleases the king, let my life be given me at my petition and my people at my request (3). Then King Ahasuerus said to Queen Esther, who is he, and where is he who dares presume in his heart to do that? (5).

And Esther said, an adversary and an enemy, even this wicked Haman. Then Haman was afraid before the king and queen. And the king arose from the feast in his wrath and went into the palace garden; and Haman stood up to make request for his life to Queen Esther, for he saw that there was evil determined against him by the king (6-7).

When the king returned out of the palace garden into the place of drinking wine, Haman was falling upon the couch where Esther was. Then said the king, Will he even forcibly assault the queen in my presence, in my own palace? As the king spoke the words, the servants covered Haman's face (8).

Then said Harbonah, one of the attendants serving the king, Behold, the gallows fifty cubits high, which Haman has made for Mordecai, whose warning saved the king, stands at the house of Haman. And the king said, Hang him on it! So they hanged Haman on the gallows that he had prepared for Mordecai. Then the king's wrath was pacified (9-10).

Based on the text, the weapon of fasting is effective! After Queen Esther exposed Haman's satanic assignment of the spirits of destruction and death against her and the Jews, there was an immediate cause of action to destroy Haman, his family, and his decree. In order to cancel the assignment of Haman, the king gave the Jews permission to defend and protect themselves and destroy any attack from the enemy (Esther 8:11). Soon after, the Jews annihilated their enemies and Queen Esther and Mordecai were exalted in great honor in the kingdom. As a matter of fact, Mordecai shifted from the gate of the king to next to the king as an ambassador for his people (Esther 10:3).

Without the weapon of fasting, none of the results for Queen Esther, Mordecai, or the Jews would have occurred. Believers of God, remember Satan is the adversary that fights against us and it is crucial to arm ourselves with the weapon of fasting. In the same manner as the king granted the Jews permission to war against their enemies, God has granted believers the power to war against Satan. Moreover, even as fasting rendered mighty results for the Jews, fasting will render mighty results for believers. Like Queen Esther and Mordecai, fasting will shift every believer that fasts from the gate to the inner court of God and from an earthly state to keen ambassadors in the spirit realm for the kingdom of God. Instead of experiencing the taunting of the agents of Satan, there is immediate vindication and honor given to us as believers to totally destroy their agenda and attacks against our lives, families, destinies, and purpose.

Chapter Six Review

1. What is fasting?

   _____

   _____

2. What does fasting require?

   _____

   _____

   _____

3. What is the purpose of the weapon of fasting?

   _____

   _____

4. What is the Holy Spirit given permission to accomplish in fasting?

   _____

   _____

5. Why is fasting so powerful?

   _____

   _____

Weapons for Spiritual Warfare   The Weapon of Fasting

6. What do believers receive from fasting?

_____

_____

7. What did God consider to be an improper way to fast?

_____

_____

8. How did God describe His chosen fast?

_____

_____

_____

9. How did Jesus state that a fast should be completed?

_____

_____

_____

10. What does Matthew 6:16 say?

_____

_____

_____

11. What did Jesus consider an outer display of fasting?

   _____

   _____

12. What does a believer lose in an improper fast?

   _____

   _____

13. According to Jesus, what is the proper way to fast?

   _____

   _____

14. Who leads a believer into a fast?

   _____

15. What does the anointing oil on our heads symbolize?

   _____

   _____

16. Why should believers wash our faces?

   _____

   _____

17. For the believer, what are the blessings of a proper fast?

___

___

18. What is the purpose of fasting?

___

___

19. What did Jesus say the disciples lacked in Matthew 17: 14-21?

___

20. What atmosphere did Jesus create to help the boy?

___

21. What weapons were needed to cast out the demon?

___

22. The demon gained ground in the boy's life because…

___

___

23. What will a fast accomplish when it is done properly?

___

___

24. What weapons were proclaimed by Jehoshaphat and why?

25. What did fasting do in the situation for Jehoshaphat?

26. What was Esther's primary weapon against the enemy's attack to her people?

27. What was the reason for the Esther's fast?

28. Where does fasting thrust the believer?

29. What did Esther receive from the king?

30. What did Esther receive from the fast?

31. What did God do for Mordecai?

32. How effective was fasting in Esther's situation?

33. How did the fast shift Mordecai's position in the kingdom?

34. How does fasting shift believers?

Chapter Seven

The Weapon of Love

And walk in love, esteeming and delighting in one another as Christ loved us and gave Himself up for us, a slain offering and sacrifice to God for you, so that it became a sweet fragrance (Ephesians 5:2, AMP Version).

Love is a major weapon in spiritual warfare that requires maturity and sacrifice. Love binds everything the Spirit of God desires to work in and through every believer together with the direct purpose and will of God for our lives. It identifies every born again believer and confirms that we are the children of God. If God's love is not evident, then God is not known (1 John 4:7-8). The premise of the Christian faith is based on the power of the love of God. Without the love of God, Satan would still have many in bondage to darkness and the influence of sin. However, God sent the weapon of love in the person of His Son Jesus on assignment (1 John 4:10). Jesus as the weapon of love became a "slain offering and sacrifice" for an ungodly world rescuing every person who believes in Him out of Satan's kingdom of darkness, from the power of sin, and placing them in the kingdom of God.

Because He knows the impact that the weapon of love makes against the stratagems of Satan, Jesus commands believers to love. The love of Jesus is the conduit for believers to flow in all weapons of warfare in the full power of the Holy Spirit against Satan. When believers wear the mature love of Jesus in our hearts and lives, faith and boldness are increased and love is a bulletproof vest repelling the spirits of fear, jealousy, and hatred.

The Mature Love of Jesus

For believers, what is mature love? Mature love is love that is perfected and developed in God by the Holy Spirit. It is a love that is sincere and without pretense (Romans 12:9). In addition, mature love is a continual work in progress. Some situations and circumstances with others are the tools to sharpen the growth. While rejecting everything love is not, mature believers put on or wear everything love is. How does a believer know love is mature within him/her? It is when he/she can love God and love others operating in what Jesus considers the greatest commandments and Paul considers the bond of perfectness.

And He replied to him, You shall love the Lord your God with all your heart and with all your soul and with all your mind (intellect). This is the great (most important principal) and first commandment. And a second is like it: You shall love your neighbor as you do yourself. These two commandments sum up and upon them depend all the Law and the Prophets (Matthew 22:37-40, AMP Version).

And above all these put on love and enfold yourselves with the bond of perfectness which binds everything together completely in ideal harmony (Colossians 3:14, AMP Version).

Flowing in Mature Love

By simply embracing through Jesus the unconditionality of God's love in our lives, we flow in mature love. This is important because believers understand He loved us first freeing us to love Him (1 John 4:19). The fruit of loving God with all our hearts produces the desire to please Him and obey everything He requires in His Word. In addition, through the love of Jesus, every believer has the propensity to love one another and others. Loving others reveals that God's presence is abiding and solidifies that His love is maturing within the life of the believer. According to the Apostle John, as love functions strongly in believers, God's presence remains stronger fulfilling a complete work within us.

Beloved, if God loved us so very much, we also ought to love one another. No man has at any time yet seen God. But if we love one another, God abides (lives and remains) in us and His love (that love which is essentially His) is brought to completion (to its full maturity, runs its full course, is perfected) in us! (1 John 4:11-12, AMP Version).

What Mature Love Does

After understanding what the mature love of God is, we must understand what the mature love of God does for believers. In the lives of believers, mature love yields a boldness to see God and the spirit of fear is expelled. As earlier stated in chapter two, fear has an assignment to paralyze and cripple believers. In addition, when love is not perfected or completely matured, fear produces torment. On the other hand, mature love in/for God expels the spirit of fear and the torment.

In this union and communion with Him love is brought to completion and attains perfection with us, that we may have confidence for the day of judgment with assurance and boldness to face Him because as He is, so are we in this world. There is no fear in love (dread does not exist), but full grown complete, perfect love turns fear out of doors and expels every trace of terror! For fear brings with it the thought of punishment and so he who is afraid has not reached the full maturity of love (is not yet grown into love's complete perfection) (1 John 4:17-18, AMP Version).

According to the Apostle John, the weapon of love is what shuts the door and totally removes the spirit of fear. As a believer, understanding the power of the operation of God's mature love as the true weapon that removes the spirit of fear and torment is vital. The reason why is fulfilling love's assignment gives believers an assurance that God is pleased with us and we are not afraid of receiving the adverse judgment of God. However, believers who do not embrace this truth have not matured in the love of God. As a result, this opens the door for the spirit of fear to attack their minds and spirits. As believers of God, it is not the will of God that the spirit of fear is allowed to torment and reign because God did not give us the spirit of fear; but, He gave us power, love, and a sound mind (2 Timothy 1:7).

Love repels Hatred

Love becomes a protective covering as an armor and bullet proof vest against the works of Satan (1Thessalonians 5:8). This vest of love repels the spirits of hatred and jealousy. Whereas it may appear that as believers our enemies are flesh and blood, love permits us to look beyond the flesh and see the demonic spirit influencing the actions. Having this knowledge gives believers the ability to perform what Jesus requested regarding our enemies. The Apostle Matthew shares Jesus' request.

> *Ye have heard that it hath been said, Thou shalt love thy neighbour, and hate thine enemy. But I say unto you, Love your enemies, bless them that curse you, do good to them that hate you, and pray for them which despitefully use you and persecute you (Matthew 5:43- 44).*

According to Jesus, when the spirit of hatred attempts to rear its head against a believer, the weapon to employ is love. Every believer will experience Satan's attempt to persecute, speak curses against his/her destiny or ministry as well as experience hatred from those who oppose the righteous stand for Jesus Christ (Mark 13:13). Despite the face attached to the attack, believers must understand that the attacks we may experience are not personal attacks, but spiritual.

How is this exposed? This is exposed through prayer. When believers are faced with such great attacks against their character, ministry, or destiny through persecution, we should pray. Believers pray for the person warring against them binding the demonic influence functioning in their lives.

While praying for the person Satan may have assigned for the spiritual attack, believers must choose to forgive the person and ask God to permit love to reign in their hearts for the person. Immediately, love will repel the assignment of Satan causing believers to love the person and hate the spirit. This response blesses the person(s) with the love of Jesus and frees them from Satan's demonic control of hatred.

As much as believers are requested to love our enemies or the enemies of God and not hate them, God is adamant regarding loving each other in the body of Christ. Believers must war against the spirit of hatred infiltrating the body of Christ against each other and apply the weapon of the love. If believers do not war against the spirit of hatred, the results are detrimental. How? When a believer states that he/she loves God and hates a fellow Christian, the Word of God connects that believer to Satan. Satan is the father of all liars. The Word of God refers to that believer as a liar not connected to God's love.

> *If anyone says, I love God and hates (detests, abominates), his brother in Christ, he is a liar; for he who does not love his brother whom he has seen, cannot not love God, Whom he has not seen. And this command, (charge, order, injunction), we have from Him: that he who loves God shall love his brother (believer) also (1 John 4:20-21, AMP Version).*

Furthermore, the spirit of hatred towards fellow Christians separates believers from God and gives place for darkness and murder to reign.

> *Whoever says he is in the Light and yet hates his brother [Christian born-again child of God his Father] is in darkness even until now. Whoever loves his brother (believer) abides (lives) in the Light, and in It*

or in him there is no occasion for stumbling or cause error or sin (1 John 2:9-10, AMP Version).

But he who hates, (detests, despises) his brother in Christ is in darkness and walking (living) in the dark; he is straying and does not perceive or know where he is going, because the darkness has blinded his eyes (1 John 2:11, AMP Version).

Anyone who hates, (abominates, detest) his brother in Christ is at heart a murderer, and you know that no murderer has eternal life abiding (persevering) within him (1 John 3:15, AMP Version).

In comparison, love is connected to the Light and hatred is connected to darkness. When believers abide in the love of God, we remain in the Light of Jesus' protection having clear direction from any occurrence of falling for any reason into sin. However, believers that hate their brethren are backslidden and unaware that darkness has gripped their hearts because they are blinded by hatred. Moreover, the hatred of the brethren is compared to the crime of murder. Remember, Satan kills, but Jesus gives life (John 10:10). Therefore, believers under the influence of the spirit of hatred are really personal assassins of Satan. For this reason, the weapon of love must be employed for the person(s) hating and to the person(s) being hated that no one perish in darkness. Only the weapon of Jesus' love has the power to change a heart of hatred to a heart of love and light.

Love repels Jealousy

Another enemy that the weapon of love repels is the spirit of jealousy. The spirit of jealousy is prideful, selfish, resentful, touchy feely, slanderous, thinks evil or the worse of people, it is envious, and it will attempt to assassinate. This is evident in 1 Samuel chapter seventeen with King Saul and David.

In 1 Samuel chapter seventeen, Israel was fighting against the Philistines. David brothers were participating in the war. David's father sent him on an assignment to bring them food and report their welfare. However, the battle did not begin until David arrived on the scene accepting the challenge to fight against the Philistine's champion Goliath. After meeting with King Saul, David proceeded into the battle. With the name of the Lord and one stone from a slingshot, David defeated Israel's enemy.

Of course, this victory provoked praises unto God and a celebration in the nation. Bear in mind, this was a victory for the nation; however, the women's song of praise for Israel's champion uncovered the spirit of jealousy in King Saul. Due to his insecurity and immaturity in jealousy, King Saul did not lead David or groom him because he saw David as competition and a threat to his kingly position.

And the women responded as they laughed and frolicked, saying, Saul has slain his thousands and David his ten thousands. And Saul was very angry, for the saying displeased him; and he said, they have ascribed to David ten thousands, but to me they have ascribed only thousands. What more can he have but the kingdom? And Saul jealousy eyed David from that day forward. Now Saul told Jonathan his son and all his servants that they must kill David (1 Samuel 18:7-9, 19:1, AMP Version).

King Saul allowed the spirit of jealousy to reign in his life against David. His jealousy drove him to view David as an enemy that should no longer exist. This is evident by the King Saul's several attempts to kill or assassinate David (1 Samuel 19:8-11, 20:30-33, 24:11).

Similar to the actions of King Saul towards David, Satan has released the spirit of jealousy on a direct assignment against the body of Christ. Even as hatred, jealousy hinders the advancement of believers in the kingdom of God. Jealousy is designed to block the destiny and purpose in the lives of the believers. Because of either their own or someone else's immaturity and insecurities, believers succumbing to the spirit of jealousy will not build or assist anyone to reach his/her destiny in the kingdom of God. Instead of celebrating their brother or sister in the Lord, believers operating in jealousy will view someone who is more anointed, gifted, or talented than they are as a threat or competition. Having the King Saul syndrome, many spiritual leaders under the influence of jealousy have damaged the lives of many believers they were assigned to groom to/for purpose. Likewise, many believers who are part of the lay body have succumb to the spirit of jealousy forgetting that every joint of the body supplies a person of edification in love (Ephesians 4:16).

Unfortunately, many believers are hurt and devastated by whomever Satan chooses to operate the spirit of jealousy through to attack them. During those moments, Satan's objective is to have the hurt person(s) to believe that the warfare is in the flesh with a person and not perceive the spirit in operation. The key to knowing the difference between the spirit of jealousy and the spirit of love is having a Godly perception of love. The spirit of love is completely opposite to the spirit of jealousy. In 1 Corinthians 13:4-7 (AMP Version), The Apostle Paul describes the spirit of the love of God as follows:

Love endures long and is patient and kind; love never is envious or boils over with jealousy, is not boastful or vainglorious, does not display itself haughtily. It is not conceited (arrogant and inflated with pride); it is not rude (unmannerly) and does not act unbecomingly. Love (God's love in us) does not insist on its own rights or its own way, for it is not self-seeking; it is not touchy or fretful or resentful; it takes no account of the evil done to it (it pays no attention to a suffered wrong). It does not rejoice at injustice and unrighteousness, but rejoices when right and truth prevail. Love bears up under anything and everything that comes, is ever ready to believe the best of every person, its hopes are fadeless under all circumstances, and it endures everything without weakening.

Based on the Apostle Paul's description, love is a powerful force against jealousy. If you are a believer experiencing warfare with the spirit of jealousy, the weapon of love is the only way to have victory. You must remember that love is not selfish, resentful, and holds no grudges. However, love is patient, kind, and believes there is still good even in the immature and insecure person(s) that Satan has blinded with the spirit of jealousy.

By embracing the protective covering of the weapon of love, you are shielded from the attacks of Satan. Remember, the spirit of jealousy has an assignment of assassination. It will attempt to kill your character with darts of lies to slander your reputation and hinder your purpose and destiny in ministry. Therefore, be armed with the weapon of love.

As a believer in the midst of being tried by the spirit of jealousy, there may be times that you may not feel like loving or forgiving; however, those are the times you must choose to love and forgive. Do not permit the spirit of jealousy to victimize you. In addition, Satan can manipulate your feelings. Therefore, as a believer operating in maturity, you choose to sacrifice your feelings to stay connected to God's presence.

In prayer, submit yourself unto God releasing unto God all the pain in your heart towards the person(s) Satan has assigned to operate in the spirit of jealousy. If there is someone specific, call the person(s) by name requesting that God's love overtake your heart towards them. At that moment, there is liberation of God's love in you for the person and a revelation for the person's need for deliverance. Although the spirit of jealousy continues to rage in them, the spirit of love in you for them is strong and sincere. While Satan displays to the person in jealousy that you are the enemy, God displays to you that Satan is the only enemy that you need to fight. Having this knowledge in prayer empowers you to take complete authority over the spirit of jealousy operating in the person's life releasing the spirit of love and victory destroying Satan's assignment.

Whether the spirit is fear, hatred, jealousy or any of their cohorts rising against believers of God, the weapon of love has delivering power and will never fail.

Chapter Seven Review

1. What does the weapon of love require?

   _____

2. How does love function in the lives of believers?

   _____

   _____

   _____

3. Who did God send as the weapon of love?

   _____

4. In what way is the love of Jesus a conduit for believers?

   _____

   _____

5. What is love described as?

   _____

   _____

6. What is mature love?

   _____

   _____

7. What does the mature love of God do?

_____

_____

8. How do believers know the operation of mature love within them?

_____

_____

9. What must be embraced to flow in mature love? Explain.

_____

_____

10. What does loving others reveal?

_____

_____

11. What does some situations and circumstances in the work of mature love produce?

_____

_____

12. How does love expel fear?

_____

_____

13. What does 1 John 4:17-18 say?

14. What does 2 Timothy 1:7 say?

15. What occurs for believers who do not embrace the truth of God's love?

16. How does love repel hatred?

17. In the spirit of hatred, are attacks personal or spiritual?

18. How is the answer to the aforementioned question exposed?

19. What should believers do when our character is attacked?

20. Who should believers hate instead of the person?

21. Who does God connect believers to that hate other Christians?

22. What does the 1 John 4:20-21 call that believer?

23. What occurs when the spirit of hatred is towards fellow Christians?

24. Hatred is considered to be what type of crime?

25. How is love and hatred compared?

26. Believers under the influence of the spirit of hatred are considered?

27. The weapon of Jesus' love has the power to do what?

28. What are the attributes of the spirit of jealousy?

29. What was David's assignment given by his father?

30. What was King Saul's problem with David and within himself?

31. Why does Satan release the spirit of jealousy against believers?

32. What is the effect of the spirit of jealousy in the lives of believers?

33. How will believers recognize the spirit of jealousy in operation?

34. Read 1 Corinthians 13:4-7. What did you gain from this passage of Scripture?

35. When believers do not feel like forgiving, what must we do?

36. Why would believers sacrifice our feelings?

37. What does God display regarding the spirit of jealousy?

Chapter Eight

The Weapon of Forgiveness

In prayer there is a connection between what God does and what you do. You can't get forgiveness from God, for instance, without also forgiving others. If you refuse to do your part, you cut yourself off from God's part. (Matthew 6:14-15, The Message Bible Version).

When believers experience disappointments, betrayals, and hurts from human interactions, Satan attempts to embed in our hearts the spirit of unforgiveness. The spirit of unforgiveness produces bitterness displaying resentment, animosity, and hostility, which can linger for years. The deception of Satan is to convince believers that there is a justifiable cause. Though unforgiveness seems justifiable on the surface, believers cannot afford to harbor unforgiveness in our hearts. The reality is the spirit of unforgiveness is an assignment from Satan to hinder the prayer lives of believers and separate us from God.

Believers must make a choice to release unforgiveness and apply the weapon of forgiveness. When choosing to let go of the pains of the past and the offenses of the present, forgiveness benefits both the person being forgiven and the person offering the forgiveness. Letting go of unforgiveness is not a matter of whose right or wrong or our feelings, it is a matter of obeying Jesus' teaching to forgive.

By applying the weapon of forgiveness, believers maintain relationship with God who empowers us to release the hurt, receive healing, personal restoration, and fulfill divine purpose. While some relationships through forgiveness may be restored or reconciled, others may not reconcile to the level of fellowshipping or engaging with the person(s) you have forgiven. As believers, we must understand that God's forgiveness does not always require that we reconcile or remain connected to the person(s) who have offended or hurt us. For all intents and purposes, what God requires is that we sincerely forgive them in obedience to His Word.

How is this done? According to the Apostle Paul, we forgive everything through Jesus Christ lest Satan should have an advantage. In addition, believers are not ignorant of Satan's devices (2 Corinthians 2:10-11). Therefore, we must not give Satan the advantage through the spirit of unforgiveness. His goal is to keep believers blind to the true warfare connected to the spirit of unforgiveness. However, every believer that understands the true warfare is empowered by Jesus to flow successfully in the weapon of forgiveness.

Jesus Operates in the Weapon of Forgiveness

Understanding the weapon of forgiveness requires understanding Jesus who forgave. As first partaker, Jesus knows exactly what it takes to operate in forgiveness. Jesus was hated without a cause by His own people (John 15:25). Before the cross, Jesus gave Himself for people that betrayed, denied, and forsook Him. Jesus understood that He was on assignment from His Father and the spirits of jealousy, murder, hatred, rejection, and betrayal were on assignment from Satan. In addition, Jesus knew the people were not aware that his crucifixion was a spiritual assignment. Therefore, while on the cross enduring the pain, Jesus requested that God the Father would forgive all the people that hurt Him exemplifying forgiveness (Luke 23:34). Jesus remained connected to His Father and focused on His divine purpose to save the world. After the cross and fulfilling His assignment, Jesus endures the rejection from an ungrateful world everyday. However, regardless of the offense, He will still forgive any and everyone who will come to Him in repentance. Jesus skillfully and victoriously operates in the weapon of forgiveness.

Having said that, believers are encouraged to forgive regardless of disappointments, betrayals, and hurt feelings. It is not because Jesus does not care about the situations affecting us. On the contrary, having gone through the process of forgiveness victoriously, Jesus is touched by every believer's experience of pain and empowers us to rise above it and forgive. This principle of forgiveness is based on the fact that because Jesus forgave us, the Jesus in every believer has the ability to forgive others. Colossians 3:13, encourages believers to forgive any quarrel as Christ forgave us.

Someone may ask, "What if this situation is reoccurring and I have forgiven this person time and time again?" In Matthew chapter eighteen, the disciples asked Jesus a similar question.

Then Peter came up to Him and said, Lord, how many times may my brother sin against me and I forgive him and let it go? As many as up to seven times? Jesus answered him, I tell you, not seven times, but seventy times seven! (Matthew 18:21-22, AMP Version).

According to Jesus, believers have the capacity to forgive four hundred and ninety times a day someone who has hurt, offended, or trespassed against us.

Not only do believers forgive, but we also let all the bitterness and anger go (Ephesians 4:31). Think about Jesus' answer to Peter and imagine how many times He forgives believers on a daily basis in order to request that we uphold such a standard. Remember, the forgiveness believers give is based on the forgiveness Jesus gave and continues to give to us. An example of this principle is given by Jesus in Matthew 18:23-35 (AMP Version).

Therefore the kingdom of heaven is like a human king who wished to settle accounts with his attendants. When he began the accounting, one was brought to him who owed him 10,000 talents [probably about $10,000,000] (23-24).

And because he could not pay, his master ordered him to be sold, with his wife and his children and everything that he possessed, and payment to be made. So the attendant fell on his knees, begging him, Have patience with me and I will pay you everything (25-26).

And his master's heart was moved with compassion, and he released him and forgave him cancelling the debt. But the same attendant, as he went out, found one of his fellow attendants who owed him a hundred denarii [about twenty dollars]; and he caught him by the throat and said, Pay what you owe! (27-28)

So his fellow attendant fell down and begged him earnestly, give me time, and I will pay you all! But he was unwilling, and he went out and had him put in prison till he should pay the debt (29-30).

When his fellow attendants saw what had happened, they were greatly distressed, and they went and told everything that had taken place to their master. Then his master called him and said to him, you contemptible and wicked attendant! I forgave and cancelled all that great debt of yours because you begged me to (31-32).

And should you not have had pity and mercy on your fellow attendant, as I had pity and mercy on you? And in wrath his master turned him over to the torturers (the jailors), till he should pay all that he owed. So also, My heavenly Father will deal with every one of you if you do not freely forgive your brother from your heart his offenses (33-35).

In this parable, Jesus expresses His heart for forgiveness as the king illustrates the principle of forgiveness to the attendant. The attendant's debt was so great that punishment was required, but grace released him to forgiveness. In comparison, the debt that the attendant's friend owed him was much smaller; yet, he did not give his friend the same grace of forgiveness the king gave him. The attendant did not understand the forgiveness lesson. Instead of embracing the grace to forgive based on his experience with the king, the attendant operated in unforgiveness. Moreover, his missed opportunity to render forgiveness to his attendant friend caused him to lose the king's grace in his own situation.

Even as the natural king was moved with compassion forgiving the attendants huge debt, King Jesus' death on the cross moved God to forgive the huge debt of sin and canceled His wrath against us. Every born again believer has a past and has made mistakes that only Jesus' love could forgive releasing the weight and the residue from us. As believers, remembering the forgiveness of Jesus towards us will assist us when forgiveness seems difficult to give to others. In addition, believers must remember that forgiveness has a divine purpose.

In Matthew 6:14-15, which is the opening scripture, Jesus explains clearly that forgiveness is vital to maintaining communication and relationship with God.

> *For if you forgive people their trespasses [their reckless and willful sins, leaving them, letting them go, and giving up resentment], your heavenly Father will also forgive you. But if you do not forgive others their trespasses [their reckless and willful sins, leaving them, letting them go, and giving up resentment], neither will your Father forgive you your trespasses (Matthew 6:14-15, AMP Version).*

Jesus addresses bitterness and anger, which are by-products of the spirit of unforgiveness. In addition, Jesus emphasizes letting go all unforgiveness to ensure God will do the same for every believer. Without rendering forgiveness, believers who have oughts in our hearts cannot fellowship with God.

Jesus instructs us to make peace then God will hear us (Matthew 5:23-24). Believers who understand our divine purpose will make peace quickly not allowing Satan space in our hearts for anger and wrath (Ephesians 4:26-27). As I stated in the opening paragraph, Satan's central purpose is to separate believers from God. Without our lifeline to God, unforgiveness will linger hindering His divine purpose in our lives. Believers who understand this choose God over unforgiveness realizing that having a relationship with God is more important than holding on to the unforgiveness toward others. This action step of forgiveness permits God to move in the situation and on the hearts of everyone dealing with the spirit of unforgiveness.

Joseph Operated in the Weapon of Forgiveness

An example of this is in the life of Joseph. If anyone should have walked in unforgiveness within his life, Joseph was justified. However, each time Joseph experienced hurt, disappointment, and betrayal, he remained in God and God vindicated his cause through the weapon of forgiveness.

In the book of Genesis beginning at chapter thirty-seven and ending at chapter fifty, believers observe Joseph's process towards forgiveness. Joseph was the first son given to Jacob by his wife Rachel. Jacob loved Joseph more than all his children and made him a coat of many colors. The father's display of favoritism towards Joseph and his dreams made Joseph's brothers hate him with jealousy (Genesis 37:3-4). Why were Joseph's dreams so significant? Genesis 37:6-11 reveals how Joseph's dreams were prophetic foreshadows of his divine destiny as a national leader.

And he said unto them, Hear, I pray you, this dream which I have dreamed: For, behold, we were binding sheaves in the field, and, lo, my sheaf arose, and also stood upright; and behold, your sheaves stood round about, and made obeisance to my sheaf (6-7).

And his brethren said to him, Shalt thou indeed reign over us? Or shalt thou indeed have dominion over us? And they hated him yet the more for his dreams, and for his words. And he dreamed yet another dream, and told it his brethren, and said, Behold, I have dreamed a dream more; and, behold, the sun and the moon and the eleven stars made obeisance to me (8-9).

And he told it to his father, and to his brethren; and his father rebuked him, and said unto him, what is this dream that thou hast dreamed? Shall I and thy mother and thy brethren indeed come to bow down ourselves to thee to the earth? And his brethren envied him; but his father observed the saying (10-11).

This passage of Scripture is important because it reveals Joseph's true enemies, which were hatred and jealousy. Remembering the spirit of jealousy from chapter eight, Satan sends the spirit of jealousy on assignment to assassinate. Once jealousy entered the hearts of Joseph's brothers, they had determined death against his destiny; however, God intervened (Genesis 37:18-20, 22, 28, 36).

And when they saw him afar off, even before he came near unto them, they conspired against him to slay him. And they said one to another, Behold, this dreamer cometh. Come now therefore, and let us slay him, and cast him into some pit and we will say, some evil beast hath devoured him: and we shall see what will become of his dreams (18-20).

And Reuben said unto them, Shed no blood, but cast him into the pit that is in the wilderness, and lay no hand upon him; that he might rid him out of their hands, to deliver him to his father again (22).

Then there passed by Midianites merchantmen: and they drew and lift up Joseph out of the pit, and sold Joseph to the Ishmeelites for twenty pieces of silver and they brought Joseph to Egypt (28).

And the Midianites sold him into Egypt unto Potiphar, an officer of Pharaoh's and captain of the guard (36).

In order to kill purpose or the dream, Satan had an assignment to kill the dreamer.

At this time, Joseph did not have the full understanding of his dreams; however, it was clear that God would not permit this situation to destroy him. Also, this would not be the last time that he would see his brothers. The reason why is because the dreams revealed that Joseph would reign over them. In addition to jealousy and hatred, another spirit revealed is betrayal. Joseph experiences a great betrayal from his brothers. First, he is tossed into a dark pit. Then, Joseph was taken away from the father he loved and sold into a foreign land. Nevertheless, Joseph remained faithful to God.

Directly after, Joseph was taken to Potiphar's house. God gave him favor with Potiphar and promoted him to a leadership position to oversee everything. Because of Joseph's connection to God, Potiphar trusted Joseph and his house was blessed. When Potiphar's wife attempted to have a sexual encounter with Joseph, this all changed. After Joseph refused her advances, she lied to her husband and falsely accused Joseph. Her actions destroyed Potiphar's relationship with Joseph. Potiphar was so angry that he placed Joseph in prison for a crime he did not commit. Nevertheless, Joseph was blessed in this outlandish life circumstance because God was still in control of his destiny.

And Joseph's master took him, and put him into the prison, a place where the king's prisoners were bound; and he was there in the prison. But the Lord was with Joseph, and showed him mercy, and gave him favour in the sight of the keeper of the prison. And the keeper of the prison committed to Joseph's hand all the prisoners that were in the prison; and whatsoever they did there, he was the doer of it. The keeper of the prison looked not to anything that was under his hand; because the Lord was with him, and that which he did, the Lord made it to prosper (Genesis 39:20-23).

Instead of functioning out of hurt and unforgiveness because he was an innocent man, Joseph maintained a forgiving heart. This is evident because God was with him and continued to give him favor. Even in the prison, Joseph operated in his divine calling to lead. Furthermore, he was an effective leader and the prison keeper trusted him without question.

As Joseph continues to reveal steps to forgiveness, his next experience of assisting the butler and baker is something all believers have experienced. In Genesis chapter forty, Pharaoh's butler and baker were thrown into prison. Each man had a dream and Joseph gifted with interpretation rendered the interpretations for both of their dreams. Joseph informed them that the baker would die and the butler would live to see Pharaoh. After assisting them, Joseph shared his testimony and requested that they remember him before Pharaoh. Upon their release, everything happened as Joseph had stated; however, Genesis 40:23 states, *"Yet did not the chief butler remember Joseph, but forgat him."*

Believers of God, have you ever assisted people who were in a low place or prison? After you walked them through their prison speaking life and deliverance, they received freedom and blessing and appeared to have forgotten about you. Even as Joseph forgave the butler, you can forgive too. The reason why is because God has an opportune time for the butlers to remember His people.

After going through disappointment, betrayal, false accusations, prison, and being forgotten, God divinely intervened on the behalf of Joseph. The only way God could do this is Joseph had to have had a heart of forgiveness. God gave Pharaoh a dream, which provoked the butler to remember Joseph. Genesis chapters forty and forty-one explains how Joseph interpretated Pharaoh's dream and was promoted into his destined leadership position right beside Pharaoh.

And Pharaoh said unto Joseph, I am Pharaoh, and with thee shall no man lift up his hand or foot in all the land of Egypt. And Joseph was thirty years old when he stood before Pharaoh king of Egypt. And Joseph went out from the presence of Pharaoh, and went throughout all the land of Egypt (Genesis 41:44, 46).

By making Joseph ruler in Egypt, God vindicated him from all the stratagems of Satan against his life. Furthermore, everything that Joseph experienced should have held him bound to unforgiveness; however, the weapon of forgiveness gave him the freedom to see that God had total control of every situation.

After God positioned Joseph as ruler of Egypt, his family faced famine and needed food from Egypt. Being unaware that Joseph was the ruler, his brothers bowed before Joseph requesting food and fulfilling the prophetic dream of Joseph's youth regarding his purpose. Obviously, God knew Joseph's heart concerning his family and permitted them to be reconciled after thirteen years. Believers of God, Joseph viewing his brothers rendered combined feelings of old pain and happiness to see them. Therefore, he had to work through the process of forgiveness to reconcile himself to his family. Once again, I would like to say, God does not always require us to reconnect to those who have wronged us in the forgiveness process. However, Joseph's reconciliation to his family was the will of God for his life.

Through his journey of forgiveness, Joseph went from being a teenage boy to becoming a thirty year old man in Egypt. He was not the same person that they had placed in the pit and sold into slavery. Having God as the consistent person in his life, afforded him the capacity to gain wisdom and spiritual clarity to why God permitted his brothers to do what they did to him. After revealing himself to his brothers, Joseph released them explaining God had a purpose and plan for his life. Genesis 45:4-5, 7-8, 15 reveals the details of the conversation:

> *And Joseph said unto his brethren, come near to me I pray you. And they came near. And he said, I am Joseph your brother, whom ye sold into Egypt. Now therefore be not grieved, nor angry with yourselves, that ye sold me hither: for God did send me before you to preserve life (4-5).*

And God sent me before you to preserve you a posterity in the earth, and to save your lives by a great deliverance. So now it was not you that sent me hither, but God: and he hath made me a father to Pharaoh, and lord of all his house, and a ruler throughout all the land of Egypt (7-8).

Moreover he kissed all his brethren, and wept upon them: and after that his brethren talked with him (15).

Joseph totally let go of the past hurts done by the hands of his brothers and was reconciled to them. Soon after their reconciliation, all of Joseph's family including his father dwelled in the land of Egypt.

After Joseph's father died, his brothers were afraid that Joseph would revenge past offenses and requested that Joseph forgive them (Genesis 50:16-17). This is an important observation in the weapon of forgiveness. As believers, you may have taken the high road and forgave people and moved on with your life totally letting go of everything; however, the people may still have guilt or suspicion in their hearts because they may not have requested that you forgive them. Due to what was in their hearts, they assumed that the forgiveness you gave was not real. Believers of God, it is unfortunate that it took the death of their father for Joseph's brothers to sincerely acknowledge their wrong.

And his brethren also went and fell down before his face; and they said, Behold we be thy servants. And Joseph said unto them, Fear not: for am I in the place of God? But as for you, ye thought evil against me, but God meant it unto good, to bring to pass, as it is this day, to save much people alive (Genesis 50:18-20).

There are two important statements in this passage of Scripture. First, God is the avenger of those who have betrayed, hurt, or disappointed us. Second, God plans are for good towards believers who trust and love Him. Even though Satan and his cohorts employ vessels for evil, God has predestined that good will come out of all the pain of being betrayed, abused, hated, disappointed, rejected, forgotten, lied on and falsely accused, dealing with dream killers, thrown in the pit of the darkness of loneliness and prison (Romans 8:28). Through Jesus, believers of God can survive all of the above to save many people's lives and reach our divine destiny.

Therefore, if there is any unforgiveness in your hearts, today is the day to let it all go. As I stated earlier, you may not want to let it go, but you must choose to let it go. As soon as you make that choice, God will move. God will give you the desire to grow from the place of unforgiveness to the place of wholeness in forgiveness. Immediately you will notice that you are not the same person or in the same place of unforgiveness where you began. In addition, you will gain the true perspective of God presence as well as spiritual clarity in the matter. Remember, if you "do your part" you will stay connected to God freeing up His hand to "do His part."

In order to take authority over the spirits of unforgiveness, anger, and bitterness, simply pray unto God allowing Him to assist/empower you to take authority and rendering healing and forgiveness. Below is an example of this action to start you on your way today:

Father in the name of Jesus, I choose to forgive (call the person(s) by name) and I ask you to assist me with your grace to fulfill this process. Jesus let your blood cleanse my being uprooting every seed sown by Satan through unforgiveness. Become a spiritual needle stitching up every wounded area in my life healing every broken place seen and unseen physically/emotionally/mentally/spiritually and seal up all the wounds forever. In the name of Jesus, I release the spirits of unforgiveness, anger, and the root of bitterness from my spirit and life. I bind the works and fruit of the operation of those spirits and send them to the pit of hell from which they come in Jesus' name. I loose the spirits of forgiveness, peace and love within me to saturate my heart and being and for (call the person(s) by name) in Jesus' name. Father in Jesus' name, I ask that you help me to see (call the person (s) by name) the way that you see him/her/them. Today, whether or not he/she receives my forgiveness or requests my forgiveness, I am letting go of the pain, person(s), situation, unforgiveness, anger, and bitterness and today I receive my complete healing to move forward. Father, because I have obeyed your Word regarding forgiveness and have done my part, I know that you will move on my behalf and do your part. Thank you in Jesus' name. Amen.

Chapter Eight Review

1. Why does Satan assign the spirit of unforgiveness?

   _____
   _____

2. Letting go of unforgiveness is a matter of?

   _____
   _____
   _____

3. According to Apostle Paul, what is Satan's plan regarding forgiveness?

   _____
   _____

4. How did Jesus operate in forgiveness?

   _____
   _____

5. What was the crucifixion?

   _____

6. What is the principle of forgiveness based on?

   _____
   _____

7. How many times should we forgive?

   _____

8. What should we let go of when forgiving others?

   _____

9. What happened in the Matthew 18 parable shared by Jesus about forgiveness?

   _____

   _____

   _____

10. The attendant did not understand what lesson?

    _____

11. What opportunity did the attendant miss?

    _____

    _____

12. What did Jesus' death move God to do?

    _____

    _____

13. Why is forgiveness vital?

    _____

14. Without a lifeline to God, what will happen to unforgiveness?

15. When choosing to let go unforgiveness, what do believers permit?

16. What is the result?

17. Why did Joseph's brothers hate him?

18. What did his dreams reveal?

19. What were the true enemies of Joseph?

20. Through the spirits of hatred and jealousy, what was Satan's assignment for Joseph?

_____

_____

21. In Joseph's story, what other spirit is revealed?

_____

22. What did God give Joseph in Potiphar's house?

_____

_____

23. Who attempted to seduce Joseph?

_____

24. What was Joseph's response?

_____

25. What was Potiphar's wife reaction?

_____

26. What was Potiphar's reaction towards Joseph?

_____

27. Who did Joseph have favor with in prison?

_____

Weapons for Spiritual Warfare   The Weapon of Forgiveness

28. What function did Joseph operate in as a prisoner?

_____

29. What gifts were manifested in Joseph in prison?

_____

30. Who did Joseph help with his gifts?

_____

31. What was Joseph's request to those who he helped?

_____

_____

32. As a believer, can you relate to Joseph's experience with those he helped?

_____

_____

_____

33. Whose dream did Joseph interpret shifting his own life?

_____

34. How was Joseph vindicated?

_____

_____

35. What did the weapon of forgiveness do for Joseph?

36. Why did Joseph's family come to Egypt?

37. How many years have passed between them?

38. How old is Joseph?

39. Did Joseph forgive his brothers?

40. What did Joseph explain to his brothers regarding God's purpose? (Genesis 45: 5-8).

41. After their father's death, why were Joseph's brothers afraid?

42. Once you have forgiven them, what is the reason why people have guilt and suspicion?

43. What does Genesis 50:22 say?

44. What are the two important statements in Genesis 50:18-20?

45. What happens when believers forgive and let go?

Conclusion

We Win!

But thanks be to God, Who gives us the victory (making us conquerors) through our Lord Jesus Christ (1Corinthians 15:57, AMP Version). Now thanks be unto God, which always causeth us to triumph in Christ (2 Corinthians 2:14a)

As soldiers in the army of the Lord of hosts (Amos 4:13), this book has given believers a road map on how to be skilled warriors. The aforementioned eight weapons on each page of this book are an arsenal set that every believer must be fully equipped with at all times. In many instances, the weapons will work cohesively together to destroy Satan's agenda, activities, and his cohorts. We must remember that Satan will be judged and he has an ultimate goal to take as many souls as he can with him to hell (John 12:31). Therefore, it is imperative that believers continue to strive skillfully and victoriously in all the weapons of warfare to oppose Satan's ultimate goal as well as advance the agenda of the kingdom of God.

Remember, while we are on this earth, believers must intentionally embrace the action and operation of the spiritual warfare as a component of our everyday lives. In addition, we must cautiously watch for Satan's attempt to deceive or downplay his kingdom's operation of darkness in this world as a normal stage of life or a normal occurrence in the situation, or the circumstance. Whether it is realized or not, many things have a spiritual operation attached to them. In view of this fact, we must remain keen in our discernment recognizing the spirits in operation and taking authority over them.

For Satan, God has declared his destiny in advance and Satan does not want any believer to be fully aware of this truth. What exactly has God declared? God has declared that Satan and his cohorts' future is to dwell forever and all eternity in the lake of fire (Revelation 20:10, 14). By knowing God's plans for Satan and his cohorts' future, believers are empowered with the full backing of the kingdom of heaven. That is why in this present life we can operate in spiritual warfare with boldness canceling the assignments of Satan and the influences of darkness against our lives, families, and the body of Christ victoriously.

Please remember, by gaining applicable knowledge of the spiritual weapons to function successfully as skilled kingdom warriors impacting the earthly and the spirit realm, Satan will attempt to apply the spirit of fear to hinder the function of spiritual warfare in your life. However, key components that will assist you to boldly operate continuously in the weapons of warfare are assurance and steadfastness in God and knowing we have the advantage.

What is this advantage for believers in spiritual warfare? The advantage is that we have received the victory in advance. As our Lord, Savior, and King, Jesus has given us the victory. Although Satan plots his schemes against believers, the Word of God assures every believer that the weapons formed against us will NOT prosper (Isaiah 54:17).

In this chapter's opening Scriptures, the Apostle Paul speaking to the church at Corinth expresses that believers are conquerors, victorious, and triumphant. He renders all glory and praise unto God who is the source of/for believers causing us to **always** avail triumphantly through Jesus in spiritual warfare. Therefore, as we function in spiritual warfare, we must understand that God is not warring with or against Satan. Satan **is a created being like us** and **he is subject to God** (Colossians 1:16). Although he has some power over the world, Jesus triumphed over him defeating him completely. Through Jesus, believers are more than conquerors and overcomers over Satan, the world that Satan rules, and his cohorts (Romans 8:37). The Apostle John reminds believers that we overcame the moment that we accepted by faith that Jesus is the Christ.

> *For whatsoever is born of God is victorious over the world and this is the victory that conquerors the world even our faith. Who is it that is victorious over (that conquers) the world but he who believes that Jesus is the Son of God (1 John 5:4-5, AMP Version).*

Glory be unto God that we are conquerors and victorious over anything produced by Satan! Therefore, skilled warriors of God continue to depend on Jesus allowing the Holy Spirit to govern your every move in spiritual warfare never forgetting that God has a predestined end result. For every believer operating in spiritual warfare, the result will always be that **WE WIN!**

Conclusion Review

1. What is spiritual warfare to believers?

   _____

   _____

2. What is this book to believers?

   _____

   _____

3. In many instances, how do the 8 weapons work?

   _____

   _____

4. What should believers watch for?

   _____

   _____

5. What is the believer's advantage?

   _____

   _____

6. Is God warring with/against Satan? Explain

   _____

7. Who must believers rely on in spiritual warfare and why?

_____

_____

_____

8. What does 1 John 5:4-5 say?

_____

_____

_____

9. What are the key components that will assist believers to boldly operate continuously in our weapons of warfare?

_____

_____

_____

10. What is God's predestined end result for believers?

_____

Notes

1. *Roger's 21st Century Thesaurus*, 3rd ed. Philip Lief Group, s.v. "warfare," accessed December 20, 2010, http://thesaurus.com/browse/warfare?

2. *Dictionary.com Unabridged*, Random House Inc, s.v. "antagonism," accessed December 20, 2010, http://dictionary.reference.com/browse/antagonism.

3. *Webster's New World Roget's A-Z Thesaurus LoveToKnow*, n.d., s.v. "earnestly," accessed July 9, 2011, http://www.yourdictionary.com/quotes/earnestly.

4. Merrill F. Unger. *Unger's Bible Dictionary* (Chicago: Moody Press, 1977), 412-413, s.v. "Ashtoreth and Baal."

5. James Orr, ed. *International Standard Bible Encyclopedia*, s.v. "intercession," accessed July 9, 2011, http://www.biblestudytools.com/encyclopedias/isbe/

6. *Merriam-Webster's Collegiate® Dictionary*, 11 ed. s.v., "indispensable," accessed May 16, 2012, http://www.merriam-webster.com.

7. *Dictionary.com Unabridged Random House Inc.* s.v., "sword," accessed April 28, 2012, http:// dictionary.reference.com/browse/sword.

8. Donald C. Stamps and John W. Adams., eds. *King James Version Life in the Spirit Study Bible* (1992; repr, Grand Rapids: Zondervan, 2005), 1405.

9. Merrill F. Unger. *Unger's Bible Dictionary* (Chicago: Moody Press, 1977), 1114, s.v. "salvation."

10. *Merriam-Webster.com*, n.d., s.v., "testator," accessed February 15, 2018, https://www.merriam-webster.com/dictionary/testator.

11. James Orr, ed. *International Standard Bible Encyclopedia*, s.v. "remission," accessed July 20, 2012, http://www.internationalstandardbible.com.

12. ibid, s.v. "redemption."

13. Merrill F. Unger. *Unger's Bible Dictionary* (Chicago: Moody Press, 1977), 345, s.v. "fasting."

To purchase autographed copies of this book please complete the enclosed form and mail to:

Angela Holloway Ministries
P.O. Box 501
Mauldin, SC 29662

Make all checks payable to: Angela Holloway

To invite Angela to preach at your church or event, please contact her by

Email: angelaholloway.ministries9@gmail.com

ANGELA HOLLOWAY MINISTRIES

Customer Information: **Shipping Address:**

Name:_____   Name:_____

Address:_____   Address:_____

_____   _____

Telephone:_____   Telephone:_____

QUANTITY	DESCRIPTION	UNIT PRICE	TOTAL
	Weapons for Spiritual Warfare: Applying Spiritual Weapons that Will Cause Mass Destruction to the Kingdom of Darkness (Revised and Expanded Version)	$25.00	
Autographed Copy To:		SUBTOTAL	
		SALES TAX	
		SHIPPING & HANDLING	2.63
		TOTAL DUE	

Please add 6% for sales tax (i.e. $1.20 (1 book), $2.40 (2 books) etc.

Please print your name or the name(s) of the person(s) who you would like me to autograph the book to clearly in the above space.

THANK YOU AND GOD BLESS!

www.ingramcontent.com/pod-product-compliance
Lightning Source LLC
Chambersburg PA
CBHW081219170426
43198CB00017B/2663